But God Has Promised

Cecil B. Murphey

Creation House
Carol Stream, Illinois

Published by Creation House, 499 Gundersen Drive, Carol Stream, Illinois, 60187
In Canada: Beacon Distributing Ltd., 104 Consumers Drive, Whitby, Ontario L1N 5T3
In Australia: Oracle Australia, Ltd., 18-26 Canterbury Road, Heathmont, Victoria 135

ISBN 0-88419-002-1
Library of Congress Catalog Card Number 76-16283
Printed in the United States of America

For the Luo people
who taught me so much.

This book is true. A few names have been changed to avoid embarrassment.

Contents

Introduction

A triumphant life on the mission field? In my naiveté I had thought so. Pictures flashed through my mind: one preaching engagement after another . . . scores of people converted at every meeting . . . Africans crowding around, begging for more teaching . . . dangers lurking but always a magnificent deliverance by God . . . yes, missionary life would be one success after another.

I grasped those ideas, I suppose, partially from the many letters of missionaries writing home; partially because I wanted life to be that way.

But fantasy and reality are often worlds apart. During our nearly six-year stay in Kenya (1961-1967), my attitudes altered drastically. I unlearned preconceived ideas; I relearned some basic truths of the faith; but most of all, I learned that God has never promised life to be easy or simple. Our family went through many painful situations—some of them I created myself—but through it all, God continued working.

The message of my book is summed up well in the following poem:

> God hath not promised skies always blue,
> Flower-strewn pathways all our lives through;
> God hath not promised sun without rain,
> Joy without sorrow, peace without pain.
>
> But God hath promised strength for the day,
> Rest for the labor, light for the way,
> Grace for the trials, help from above,
> Unfailing sympathy, undying love.

Annie Johnson Flint, "What God Hath Promised," *The Treasury of Religious Verse* (New York: Pyramid, 1962), P. 59. Used by permission of Evangelical Publishers.

1
A Hard Lesson

"This has to stop, Efraim! I warn you, I won't tolerate your interference again!"

The African teacher glared at me with an attempt at masked expression, but the pupils of his eyes became tiny points and his facial muscles tightened. I saw the veins in his slender neck rise, his mallet-like fists clenched involuntarily.

"You know the rules," I continued, my voice growing louder and more shrill. "As headmaster of the school you have charge over our girls only during school hours. You know that perfectly well. At all other times—and I mean *all* other times—they come under the jurisdiction of the mission. You are not allowed on the dormitory complex—no man is without permission—and you've been informed of that rule countless times."

I felt my body tighten as I continued glaring at him. *"Is that clear?"*

"Why do you treat me like this?" Efraim protested. "Do you not realize I am the headmaster of the school?" His right eye, which was crossed, made his angry face look almost ludicrous. He leaned closer as he spat out his words.

"Just a minute!" I interrupted. "You ask why?"

I could not seem to hold back the flush of anger welling up within. "Our interest is in protecting these girls. Every year three or four are dismissed because of pregnancy. It's pretty well accepted that the male teachers are responsible. So, let's get this straight—" I glared and tapped his chest with the index finger of my right hand. "You do *not* ask girls to your house at any time, for any purpose. They come to the school building *only* during school hours. I've been here less than four months but you've already given me a lot of trouble and we've reached the breaking point, Efraim!"

He knocked my hand back, spun around and stalked from my porch without a word. I watched him leave and could feel myself shaking. This was not the way to treat people, I knew.

"Lord, maybe I'm wrong, I don't know. I've become so agitated over repeated violations of the rules, I just lost my temper."

My gaze followed Efraim's thin figure across the mission station. He reached the dirt road which ran from the main road down to the bottom of the hill. The road, seldom used except by educational vehicles going down to the school to take supplies or an official to visit for inspection, was little more than two ruts with grass sprouting up between.

Efraim turned right. On his left stood a row of thatched houses. The walls had been freshly re-mudded only weeks before to patch up breaks and cracks caused by rain. Efraim lived in the last house, the closest to the modern brick school building.

"Well, that's settled," I sighed as I went back into the house. It took awhile before my emotions settled down.

That was Friday. Saturday came with its normal routine. The eighty girls in the dormitory arose early and did their chores quickly. Once finished they knew that the rest of the day would be their own.

One group of girls took pails and brought up water from the river which ran two hundred feet below the school building. Four girls skipped across the open fields to collect firewood for the coming week. Within an hour they would return, bundles of dead limbs on their heads. They never cut up live trees, but searched for dead, dried limbs and branches.

Other girls swept the dormitory, then washed down the cement floor. One group weeded or picked sweet potatoes and beans in the *shamba*.

By noon, green uniforms hung on hedges and tree limbs to dry. Later they would be pressed with charcoal-heated irons. These uniforms—which every school had—were plain green, cut and sewn by the girls themselves during their first two weeks of the school year. No girl dared enter a classroom without a uniform after the second week of school. If she attempted to enter, the teacher would make her stand outside—the worst possible punishment.

Most of the girls came from the Luo tribe, the second largest of Kenya. Many were teen-agers. Commonly we found sixteen year olds in the fifth or sixth standard (grade). One girl, we heard, was actually twenty. Girls started school much later in Kenya.

The dormitory, a concrete-block building covered with a thin cement plaster and several coats of whitewash, gleamed in the equatorial sun. Beside it stood the cook house, also cement block and whitewashed. Inside, cement blocks formed two open fireplaces where the girls cooked their own food each day. Below the cook house stood a thatch and mud building, whitewashed, but used only when we had too many girls for the permanent building and needed overflow space.

Maybe, I thought the following Sunday afternoon, *things will be better now. Efraim got the message and he'll stop sending for girls to visit his house or the school after hours.* In my few months in Kenya, I'd learned one thing: the word of a teacher is absolute. If he told a student to come to his house, regardless of propriety, the student went without hesitation. Students had extreme loyalty to their teachers, even feared them.

Evening came, time for the worship service in the girls' dormitory. My wife Shirley, as headmistress of the dorm, conducted the program. Eunice Princic, an older missionary living at Suna Mission, assisted her. "Auntie Princic," as we affectionately called her, played the guitar, occasionally preached, acted as first-aid consultant, taught needlework, held two daily Bible classes and made herself useful in many ways with the girls.

But tonight Shirley could not go. She lay in bed with the chills and fever of malaria.

I walked slowly down the winding path to the dormitory. Suna Mission sprawled down the side of Nyabisawa mountain. Larger mountains rose in the background, crested in the evenings by flaming sunsets and in the mornings by the breath-taking hues of sunrise. The unfenced vistas gave me a sense of freedom. Even though the area around Suna is semi-arid, we had lush vegetation. Papaya trees formed a border between the dormitory section and the brick house, and poinsettia bushes, five or six feet high, swayed behind the trees. Pineapples, bananas and avocados were all bearing well. A winding row of pink and white frangipani bushes caught my attention, and I paused momentarily to smell the fragrance.

I entered the dormitory and noticed immediately that at least a dozen girls were missing. "Where are they? What's happened? Where's Damar, the head prefect?" I demanded.

"Sir," a Maragoli girl mumbled, her head lowered, "the headmaster called all the standard eight girls to the school building. As you know, they will soon sit for their K.A.P.E."

"We'll see about that!" I snapped, angry that Efraim had deliberately disobeyed my recent ultimatum. I stalked from the building, slammed the door and practically ran to the bottom of the hill where the brick building stood, illuminated by the dying rays of the sun. Powdery red dust settled on my freshly polished shoes. Even the cooling breezes of evening did nothing to cool my anger.

In two weeks the students in the eighth grade would be taking their final examinations, called at that time, "Kenya African Pupils Examination." These were nation-wide and competitive; the results would determine which students entered high school the following year. It meant a great deal to these students because their entire educational future depended on the results of a single examination. It could not be repeated.

"But the religious part means a great deal, too!" I boiled as I headed for that school building. Efraim and I had tangled over this several times. Both Shirley and I had tried to make our positions clear. We knew we had not only the authority of the mission behind us, but the educational department as well. I was set for a showdown.

Through the small panel of windows in the building I could see Efraim standing facing the board, his back to the class, while every student busily wrote in a notebook. The girls sat on crude wooden benches. Across the room, eight or nine boys who were day students, also scratched away with pencils, working out problems for a lesson in mathematics.

I kicked open the door and yelled, "Efraim! Come out here!"

A shocked look on his slender face disappeared almost immediately. "Continue on, pupils," he said as he walked rapidly toward me.

"What do you mean, humiliating me in front of my pupils? Am I an animal that you order me around? I was teaching and you rush in and demand me to come out!" His chin jutted forward and his crossed-eye jiggled nervously.

"You know why I called you out! Just two days ago I told you for the last time—*you have no right*—no right whatsoever to take these girls from the dormitory without special permission. You know that! If you insist on acting underhandedly, I'll treat you like some kind of animal."

Anger glazed his eyes. "You! You!" He sputtered, drawing back.

I saw the fist coming at me, felt it crack with bone-jarring force on my left cheek. My glasses flew off and I went reeling backwards. I must have hit the back of my head on the gravel walk.

Suddenly the boys from the classroom were on top of me, pummeling and kicking. It was nearly dark and they had brought a kerosene lamp with them to the school. One of the boys grabbed the lamp, unscrewed the lid, and doused me with the pungent kerosene.

"Set him on fire!" yelled one of the boys.

Girls screamed in the background. I heard shuffling feet but I couldn't open my eyes. I could only lie there, hearing what was happening, yet unable to move or to resist.

"Oh, God, help me!" I cried, whether audibly or not, I don't know. No one now kicked or pounded me. I lay there, engulfed by darkness in my mind, unable to force my eyes open, yet acutely conscious of the slightest sounds.

One girl began sniffling; another pleaded shrilly, "Don't! Don't!"

"A match! Bring a match!" demanded a youthful male voice. "Bring a match and I will set him on fire."

A lot of muttering and shuffling went on, then I heard several voices answer, *"Onge,"* (none).

In those few seconds of searching for a match, they must have realized what they had done. This was November of 1961, two full years before independence. British rule and white power still dominated East Africa. Voices had begun crying out for "Uhuru," (independence) but white power still made the rules, still enforced them, and Africans cringed at that power.

For what seemed a long time, the world stood still and everyone froze in place. No one said anything, or perhaps I lost consciousness. Then, slowly, I opened my eyes and could see horrified faces peering down at me.

Weakly, I rose to my feet, feeling nauseous and dizzy. I touched my left cheek where I felt biting pain, and wiped blood away. The top of my head throbbed. Automatically I reached up and felt the sticky blood there, too. Later I discovered three gashes on my left cheek, the deepest nearly two inches long, cuts on the bridge of my nose, several bruises and cuts on my legs where I had been kicked, and two large bumps on the back of my head.

"Efraim! You've had it now! You've really gotten yourself in trouble and the school boys, too!"

I looked around at the hastily retreating figures of the boys. Without conscious thought they had taken the part of their teacher. Now they were in a dilemma because they had harmed a white man—a symbol of law and rule in East Africa.

Efraim and I were alone, facing each other. For the first

time I felt fear clutching at me, not knowing what he would do next, knowing only that I could never defend myself if he attacked again.

"You're through, Efraim! I'll see that you never teach again!" I screamed at him, but the teacher didn't move. He must have realized the seriousness of his predicament.

He turned then and walked dazedly toward his house. I became conscious of how unmercifully my head ached. I stooped down to pick up my glasses. A wave of blackness swept over me and I nearly passed out. I clutched at the glasses and slowly rose to my feet. The left lens was broken in small pieces, the right cracked across the middle. Still clutching the useless glasses, I staggered up the hill.

So this is Kenya, I thought. The land where God called me to preach and share the good news. I've been in the country less than four months and already have been nearly killed.

Ironically, I began to realize that I had come to teach Africans how to live for Jesus Christ. But first... *first I had a lot of learning to do myself.*

> God hath not promised sun without rain,
> Joy without sorrow, peace without pain . . . .

2

Beginnings

Where had it all started? When had I decided to become a missionary?

After high school I enlisted in the Navy. During that time the girl I loved broke off our relationship. Her words played in my head over and over and over. "This is it, Cec. I tried so hard . . . you're a wonderful guy . . . but it won't work . . ."

"Let's give it another try. Please," I pleaded.

"There's someone else." The final words. It was over.

I hadn't thought about God since Sunday School days as a child. God? He was something people talked about to soothe their consciences. But now in my grief, my thoughts kept searching Him out. I needed help.

Finally I prayed, "God, if You exist, help me. Take away the pain."

Then one night, months later, I stepped inside a military chapel at Great Lakes Naval Training Center. Twenty years old, and nothing to look forward to.

I picked up a free New Testament. Later, in the barracks and at my office I began to read. Sometimes a whole chapter; other days only a verse or two. After several weeks, I read whole books at a single sitting.

I had found God!

Through the reading of the New Testament God's love gradually unfolded. He convicted me of my sins, assured me of forgiveness. The transformation of Cec Murphey began taking place.

Over a period of months the certainty of God's existence had grown. At last I could say, "I believe." And from there, the next step, "God, I'll follow You anywhere."

From that commitment grew the increased certainty that the Lord had called me to preach the Gospel.

That same year, 1954, not only did I discover the reality of Jesus Christ, I met the next most important person in my life, Shirley Mae Brackett. Although she had seen me attending Immanuel Baptist Church in Waukegan, Illinois, a few miles from the naval base, we had never met.

During a week of special meetings that fall, I arrived late one evening and the only vacant seat was next to Shirley. At the end of the service we started a conversation, the beginning of an enduring romance.

I learned later that Shirley had also just broken up a budding romance. Both of us, still strangers to each other, had prayed a similar prayer, "God, if you want me to get married, send the right one."

Shirley, nearly as tall as I, with beautiful titian-red hair and clear blue eyes, was the most consecrated Christian I'd ever met. Her knowledge of the Bible astounded me, her closeness to Jesus Christ filled me with godly envy. She sought God's will in everything.

Our backgrounds were so different, but our desires so similar. She had known the reality of the Christian faith from early childhood. Her parents loved God themselves and carefully nurtured her in the faith, always taking her to church. I, on the other hand, had not been to church or had much to do with religion from the age of twelve. Then at twenty, I began feeling the need for some answers in my life.

The answers began coming in the person of Jesus Christ. The foul-mouthed, boozing sailor became a new person in Jesus Christ.

"Being a Christian is so wonderful," I remember saying to a friend, "I've really found everything I've been looking for. I'm content."

Now as a Christian I wanted God's will for my life. I thought about the ministry. I thought about the mission field, but not much.

The missionary type? It certainly wasn't Cec Murphey!

A missionary is an utterly capable person who preaches like Paul, loves with the compassion of John, works with one's hands like a top-grade mechanic and who has a special capacity for living in a foreign culture. He exemplifies patience and self-control. No missionary life for me!

"But Lord," I prayed sincerely, "I'll go wherever you want me to go." I didn't reject missionary work; I didn't consider it an option.

After Shirley and I married and after my discharge, I entered Bible college. During chapel services, dozens of missionaries came through, pleading for workers for the harvest field—for Japan, Indonesia, South America, and Africa.

Shirley and I listened along with the rest of the student body, prayed like the others that God would speak to us if He wanted us on the mission field. Was I not listening? Had I already made up my mind?

One of my classmates planned to go to Japan, another to Mexico. Talk of missions continually filled the air. I always maintained, "I can serve God better in this country."

So why did I become a missionary? Of course, God called me, but other forces entered in.

Did Arthur Dodzweit influence me? At the time I was not aware of his doing so. Arthur had come home from the mission field because of his wife's serious thyroid problem. He became the pastor of Lakeshore Tabernacle in Kenosha, Wisconsin, ten miles north of our home.

In a two-year period Arthur became a special person to me, more of a pastor than I had ever known before. Tall, heavy-set, he spoke with a deep voice, perpetually strained from years of loud preaching. He had light brown hair, now sprinkled with gray, and blue eyes.

Arthur radiated a special love for people. That love brought us together initially. Shirley had started down a concrete flight of stairs. Somehow she lost her balance and fell. I found her at the bottom, half-conscious, her vision blurred. Frantically, I gathered her up and laid her on the bed. I dropped to my knees and began to pray. A relative who attended Lakeshore Tabernacle called Arthur. He arrived half an hour later.

"I'll stay here and pray with you until the Lord heals Shirley," he said.

We knelt beside the bed and after concerted prayer for nearly an hour, Shirley sat up and said, "I feel fine. A warm glow came over me and I'm all right now."

That was how he became special to us. Later we began attending his church. The Dodzweits often spoke of East Africa the way one speaks of a childhood home, or a special place he has lived. But they never pushed, never urged anyone toward the mission field.

Two years of Bible college sped by. Wandalyn made her entrance into the world, increasing our family to three. Cecile (whom we called C-C) followed fifteen months later. That ended my Bible studies. I would have to get a job and support my family.

An opening came for a sixth grade teacher in Waukegan, a suburb of Chicago. A short time after I signed the contract, I was shopping in the Loop district. As I crossed a street I glanced up at a theater marquee—an unusual thing because I had not been inside a movie theater for more than five years.

In foot-high black and red letters this sign grabbed my attention:

Van Heflin and Ruth Roman
in
TANGANYIKA

Tanganyika meant little to me. Arthur Dodzweit had mentioned the country several times. I knew that geographically it bordered Kenya and was an equatorial country on the east coast of Africa. Other than that, it was only an odd-sounding name.

"You're going there," whispered an inner voice.

Me?

The thought startled me. I stared again at the gawdy marquee. Me? To Tanganyika?

I prayed about this strange experience the rest of the afternoon, even skipping my afternoon class at the teachers' college. I marshaled every reason why I couldn't go. But even as I argued with the Lord, an inner certainty began taking hold. Able or not, God would send me!

That evening I shared the news with Shirley. She took it calmly but not enthusiastically. In her characteristic way, she smiled, kissed me and said, "I'll pray about it, Cec, but it just doesn't seem right—at least not yet."

We knelt together and talked to God about Africa, but

no further light came. We agreed no decision would be made unless both of us felt Africa was God's choice for us. Shirley prayed for God's answer to that question for many months.

I wrote to several missionary organizations, but nothing productive came of the inquiries. As the days wore on, thoughts of missionary service receded into the background. For nearly two years nothing came from heaven about missionary activity. On the few occasions I thought about the foreign field, I tended to dismiss the idea that God had used a theater marquee to call me.

The only problem was, every now and then the sense of that call came back strongly. The conviction would grab me and I'd pray, "Okay, Lord, I'm ready and willing, now it's up to You."

During those two years I took courses at the teachers' college one or two evenings a week and spent all day Saturday in classes as well. I taught school and remained active in the church where Arthur Dodzweit pastored. In June of 1959 I earned my bachelor's degree.

Then an opportunity came for me to teach at Chicago Bible College three days a week. Although the pay was less than $130 a month, the new job was a step in the right direction—giving myself to the ministry of the Gospel. I did substitute work in local public schools around Waukegan on Mondays and Fridays.

I loved the work at the Bible college and felt a wonderful sense of rapport with the rest of the staff and the students. I envisioned staying there a long time. That was not to be. When the spring of 1960 rolled around I knew my days were almost at an end at the school, but didn't know why.

"Honey," I shared with Shirley, "I have this . . . this feeling . . . and that's the best I can describe it . . . this feeling I'm not to return to the college this fall. I'm not sure what comes next, only this intensely positive certainty I should not return."

We had been driving home from grocery shopping and our voices grew silent. Our two girls in the back seat seemed to hush at that moment. Baby John Mark, less than four months old, lay peacefully in the car bed.

We prayed silently as I drove. Minutes later Shirley touched my arm and her tear-filled blue eyes gazed into mine. "I think it's time to prepare for Africa."

Time to move forward. The go-ahead sign from the Lord.

The Dodzweits had returned to Kenya the previous year and we didn't even have their address.

Not knowing what else to do, I wrote to Arthur's mission, Elim Fellowship.

The reply was courteous, noncommittal but informative. No, they had no present need for missionaries in Tanganyika, although they did have churches which had sprung up across the border from Kenya. However, Elim *did* need a family at Suna Mission in Kenya.

They enclosed forms for us to fill out, "in case you're interested in pursuing this further."

"It seems right to me," Shirley nodded.

I completed the forms immediately and returned them the same day by airmail special delivery. "If it's worth doing," I said to my wife, "it ought to be worth doing fast!"

Less than a week later the mission wrote a second time. "Your prompt reply makes us feel you're really serious."

They had gotten my message.

Shortly afterward the head of Elim Fellowship, Carlton Spencer, asked me to meet with him. He would be attending a missionary convention at a church in Chicago.

I found him in the foyer of the church—a distinguished-looking man with a joyful smile. I liked him immediately.

Along with Carlton stood a young man in a black suit. His dark skin and black hair matched the suit. *Probably Italian or French,* I thought.

"This is Lee Nelson, a recently appointed missionary who's on his way to Bukuria Mission with his family. That's where the Dodzweits worked for nearly twelve years. Dodzweits are now based in Nairobi and we need this family at Bukuria. They hope to leave in a few months."

Lee and I greeted each other and chatted briefly. He had a Canadian accent.

The three of us sat in a nearly deserted room and talked well over two hours. Carlton explained the mission policy, "Elim does not underwrite the support of its missionaries. If God calls a man, then God provides. If we step in, we might actually hinder what God tries to do."

My enthusiasm for the mission grew.

"Cec, I'd like to meet your wife," Carlton said. "Is it possible while I'm here? Could she come into Chicago this evening or could we go there? I have to drive back east in the morning; this may be my only chance for a long time."

"Sure," I blurted, "I'll call her and tell her you and Lee are coming home with me for supper."

Shirley answered the phone. I shared the briefest details and added, "We're leaving now. I'm bringing both of them home for supper."

The silence was so long I wondered if we'd been cut off.

"What's wrong, Shirley?"

"Fine, bring them . . ." but her voice didn't convey that impression. "Okay, Cec, only I don't know what to serve them. I've got a half-pound of hamburger, some cheese, and that's about all." She sounded almost ready to cry.

"Oh, you'll think of something," I answered cheerily. "I—I've already invited them."

Her voice cracked and then she said, "Okay, bring them. I'll work out something."

My salary of $130 at the Bible college, even for 1960, wasn't much. Nearly a quarter of that monthly check went for gas to drive back and forth.

When I had accepted the position at the college, Shirley and I made a pact with God. "If You provide for our needs, we'll concentrate on doing Your will. You handle the finances and we'll do the trusting.

But that afternoon as I drove Lee and Carlton to our home, I wondered what we'd have on the table when we got there. I prayed that neither of them had big appetites. Four adults, two daughters, ages three and four, and a son now nearly a year old—just how far does half a pound of hamburger stretch?

While the guests washed their hands, I looked quizzically at my wife. Our eyes met and she nodded that it was all right.

The cheese had been melted, mixed with the hamburger and an onion, and made into a kind of sauce which we poured over cornbread. We had milk to drink but no dessert. The real proof of ingenuity was the salad. Shirley had picked dandelion greens out of the front yard, cut them up and spread on homemade mayonnaise.

Later I drove Lee and Carlton back to Chicago. Lee and I talked a few minutes while Carlton was busy elsewhere.

"You know what he said to me when we got ready to leave your house?"

"No," I wondered—and dreaded.

Lee smiled and said, "Carlton tapped me and whispered, 'That's the couple for Suna Mission. Any family that can eat like that and they haven't yet reached the mission field—they'll have no trouble adjusting.' "

I've often wondered if dandelion salad prepared our way to Kenya!

3
Money Problems

Later, in Carlton's office he spelled out our financial needs. $5,000? Carlton's words pierced my brain and my mind went numb. We didn't even have $50!

"Yes, $5,000, we feel, is the minimum," he continued. "Let me break that down for you. Transportation to Kenya for a family of five runs nearly $2,000. Besides that, you'll need furniture . . ." He took out a ballpoint pen and jotted figures on a slip of paper. "And a car. We also require a minimum of $500 deposit on your return fare before you leave. So you see, that's not an unreasonable figure for a family of your size."

"Well, nothing's impossible with the Lord!" I quipped.

Raising $5,000 was as difficult for me as $5 million. But we determined not to ask Elim to help. They were assisting Lee Nelson raise his so he could leave for Kenya.

We had no savings; and no one in the family or circle of friends was likely to hand us a large sum of cash.

"Lord, this is Your problem," I prayed as I stumbled out of Carlton's office. "You called us to the mission field and we're willing if You make the way."

The complexity of the situation hit me. Once we had raised the money, that only got us to the mission field! In addition, we needed a minimum of $240 every month for support.

"Lord, if You're in this, You'll work it out," Shirley prayed confidently.

We had many things to learn about God's promises. He never promises to do everything for us, nor to make the way easy. And we had not yet realized how much God intends for us to use common sense.

Through contacts at the Bible college, I knew fourteen pastors who would surely welcome us to speak at their churches. In a burst of enthusiasm I hauled out the ancient Underwood typewriter and banged out fourteen letters. By noon they were sealed and deposited in the mailbox. Then we anxiously waited for the replies. A week. Two weeks. Three. On the twenty-third day, one response came from a pastor in Michigan.

> Sorry, Cec, but I'm booked up solid for the summer and even until after Christmas. Hope you can line up meetings with the other churches.

The other thirteen never answered.

Shirley and I spent much time in prayer. To support the family I tutored in remedial reading and after school opened, substituted.

After a barren month, my red-headed wife balked. "This is enough. Are we going to sit around day after day and wait for God to do it? Maybe it's time for us to act."

"We're praying," I mumbled sheepishly.

"Then perhaps it's time to do something else!"

"Like what?" I asked, unable to think of a single thing.

"I'm going to ask Brother Broker for help."

I gasped. "Why him? We hardly know him! That's awfully presumptuous!"

"Because he's the only one I know who can and might help. No one at the college seems interested; your ministerial friends haven't even bothered to answer the letters." Her blue eyes flashed and I knew she had made up her mind.

Shirley grabbed the phone and dialed Rev. O. F. Broker's office. "Could I—could I come over and talk to you?"

He apparently agreed and she said, "I'll be there within fifteen minutes."

After the Dodzweits went back to Africa, O. F. Broker had become the pastor of Lakeshore Tabernacle. We had attended only a few times since his coming, as we were helping in a youth program in a small church two blocks from home.

Two hours later Shirley returned, her steps firm and her face triumphant.

"He gave me two contacts—just like that. One of them is Harold Meyers in Keokuk, Iowa, who publishes a monthly magazine. The other is a pastor in southern Illinois.

I got on the phone. The pastor in Illinois said he was busy, but we made a date for May—eight months in advance. My spirits lifted.

I called Harold Meyers. His deep, sonorous voice came over the phone, "We're having an all-day youth rally the last Saturday in September in Kirksville, Missouri. You can spend the night with us and preach in Keokuk Sunday morning at a small church I'm now pastoring. I'll even try to line up churches for you in this area."

From that phone call, the way unfolded slowly. Harold and his wife, Lucille, opened the doors to many churches, to their own home, and more significantly, to their very hearts. His intervention became the single most significant factor in our getting to Africa.

Harold and Lucille Meyers were the first of many strangers to open their doors to us. The first . . . but there would be others. We were learning that "our sufficiency is of the Lord" (2 Corinthians 3:5).

Even after meeting the Meyers and arranging the first preaching services, obstacles appeared unexpectedly, for money didn't come in fast; also we had physical setbacks.

Worst of all, our friends didn't understand.

We had boldly announced, "We're going to Africa as missionaries." Instead of encouraging us, they did their best to dissuade us.

A relative, himself not a church member, asked bluntly, "Why go to Africa? Aren't there enough heathen here?"

I stared into his dark eyes. "Yes, but they've heard the message all their lives and done nothing about it. Now I'm going to people who will listen."

He never argued with me again.

It was winter. Shirley became ill. It developed into pneumonia and she suffered a miscarriage while 250 miles from home. I drove her back to our apartment in Zion and stayed with her three days. Then I left for scheduled missionary meetings in northwestern Iowa.

Some of our Christian friends came to help after I left. They cleaned the apartment, cooked food, helped take care of baby John Mark and Cecile, now three. Wandalyn traveled with me to ease Shirley's burden and to make me a little less homesick.

When I returned two weeks later, Shirley had improved physically and could do her own housework, but she was upset.

"They did everything possible to make me comfortable," she said, "and I don't know what I would have done without them. But all the time they kept saying, 'See, God's showing you He doesn't want you on the mission field. It'll get worse if you don't repent and get back to God's will again.' "

I held Shirley in my arms as she sobbed out the tears she had been holding back for two weeks. Hot anger flushed through me. "Who are they to set themselves up as the voice of the Lord?"

"Cec, they love us. Maybe they're afraid we'll be hurt or killed—I don't know, but they do care about us." Her voice cracked again.

I bristled. "Do you call that love?"

" 'He who loves father or mother more than Me—' " Shirley began quoting and then stopped with a sob. "Perhaps for the first time in my life I know what that verse means."

Yet doors opened wider and more frequently as one contact led to another. God taught us valuable lessons about money, people, and churches.

In June of 1961, Shirley and I traveled to the mountains of Pennsylvania to help a young preacher, Ken Bennett, in a week of evangelistic meetings. Ken rented a tent for a week and set it up in an open field.

During that week he and I both preached, prayed and visited countless homes. Still the attendance remained low, and the offerings even smaller. At the end of the week, Ken did not have the seventy-five dollars to pay for the rental of the tent.

When we finished the week, Ken's tall blonde figure

slumped out of the tent. He dragged himself across the field, his head low.

I followed him. "Look," I said, "it's not all that bad!"

"I—I had hoped . . . prayed . . ." his voice broke as he turned away. "Prayed we'd reach a lot of people through this tent ministry. Guess it just didn't work out and now the offerings won't even pay expenses."

"Here," I said, thrusting $8.23 into his hand. "It's what you need to pay the seventy-five dollars."

He grimaced. "Now I feel even worse. I invited you, hoping to raise money for you to go to Africa and now you end up giving *me* an offering."

"Strange, isn't it, how God works?" I countered.

A woman preacher in eastern Iowa contacted us several times for a missionary service. "Just tell me when you can come and we'll arrange a meeting."

We passed through her town on our way to see my parents in Davenport. Saturday night was our only clear evening. I hesitated because most churches seldom arrange services for Saturday.

But when I called she said, "Saturday is fine!"

"You can expect us about five-thirty."

By four-thirty on Saturday we stood at her front door. "Hope you don't mind our arriving a little early," I said. "Didn't take as long on the road as we had expected."

"No . . . no, of course not," she replied without enthusiasm. "You and the youngsters must be tired. I have a nice room where you can all lie down until supper."

We followed her into a room with two twin beds. Shirley and I stretched out on one and the children sprawled contentedly on the other. For thirty minutes.

"Mommy, I'm hungry," Wandalyn whispered.

"Me, too," cooed three-year-old C-C.

"Lie quietly, kids," I whispered back. "They'll call us

when it's ready."

"But I'm not tired," C-C grouched.

"Shhh," Shirley warned.

In a few minutes we heard sounds in the kitchen and the aroma of fried chicken crept into our room. I sighed with the distinct clink of tablewear, followed shortly by scraping sounds of chairs on the floor, and of people eating.

"Did they forget about us?" Wandalyn pouted.

"They'll call us soon. Just relax."

Minutes later we heard the noise of dishes being cleared away, scraped and washed. Shirley and I glanced at each other in silence.

Just before dark, someone tapped gently on the door. "Are the Murpheys awake in there?" the woman pastor called.

"Yes, we are!" Wandalyn yelled and hopped to the floor.

"Me, too," echoed C-C.

Our hostess opened the door. "Let me show you around a little and then we can have supper." She showed us their extensive property, including luxurious handmade furniture, a new car, modern farming equipment and a large farm. She preached; her husband farmed and operated a business in town.

Apparently he supports them well, I thought.

"Come to the table and I'll set it for you," she chirped. "We only have thirty minutes before service."

She placed a small bowl of soup on the table with five smaller bowls. "Being missionaries, I imagine you don't eat much. There's more soup if you're still hungry," she called as she retired to another room while we ate.

Thirty minutes later, four people came to the service. "I'm sorry there are so few people tonight, Brother Murphey," the woman whispered as the two of us were seated on the platform. "Our other three members are out of town."

I grinned a bit, nodded and then reminded myself I

had promised God to preach my best no matter how small the audience.

Immediately after I spoke, the woman's husband passed the plate. "This offering tonight," he said, "is for the Murphey family to help them reach Africa."

As she bade us goodnight, she dumped the contents of the offering plate into my hand. I put the fifty-three cents in my pocket. "Would you like the mission board to send you a receipt?" I said dryly.

"Not necessary, Brother, we just give to the Lord and don't blow off about it," she said with a benevolent smile.

The following week, another church gave us a check for twenty-five dollars which I joyfully deposited in the bank. Shortly afterwards I received a notice from the bank with the check, and stamped across the front were two words in bold, green letters, *Insufficient Funds.*

"The idea!" I fumed, "Are they trying to cheat God?"

On another occasion the Meyers arranged for a week of meetings in a prestigious church in central Illinois. For six nights I preached. The only time I saw the pastor was when he sat on the platform during the service.

We were to stay on the third floor of a house next door to the church. By midday the heat had become so stifling, we had to go outside until the evening breezes came. For furnishings we counted two saucepans, one stove burner that worked, five plates, an assortment of unmatched tableware, and a variety of jars and small glasses. We found adequate bedding, two mattresses, but no beds.

"We're getting our missionary training in the States, aren't we?" Shirley remarked.

The pastor usually chatted with us two or three minutes immediately before the meeting and then a hasty, "See you later," at the end. "Don't you worry, Brother Murphey, we're backing you all the way. We believe in taking care of missionaries at this church!" he promised.

At the end of the week, the minister handed me a check. "This is for preaching. It's not a lot but I'll be sending you another seventy-five through your mission headquarters."

The check was for twenty-five dollars.

He also made me a business offer. He had written a pamphlet on what he believed to be truths of the end time and the fulfillment of prophecy. "These sell for one dollar; but I'll let you have them for forty cents each. In your meetings tuck your prayer card inside, sell the books for a dollar and make sixty cents profit."

With a smile that covered half his face, he asked, "How does that sound?"

"Brother, the Lord sent me to preach the Gospel, not to sell books!" I growled.

We never heard from that church again.

Two days later I preached at a small, rural church in a central Iowa farming community. The town was so small I could not find it on my map and had to phone for directions. Eleven people attended.

The pastor, a part-time preacher and a full-time farmer, told the congregation: "We're going to take an offering. I want you to give what you can to help this family to the mission field. Dig deeply."

I hadn't expected much. Not only because of my previous experiences, but during the early part of the service I had looked at the plainly dressed farmers. Yet I felt a rapport with them. As I preached, they seemed eager to listen. Somehow the Holy Spirit worked in our hearts, and I remember thinking, *this is the best service in a long time.*

When the pastor handed me the offering, he said apologetically, "We're a small church and most of the members don't have much. We only wish we could do more. Later on, maybe we can."

He gripped my hand and I knew he meant every word. I

glanced at the offering which consisted of a few one dollar bills and a handful of change. It totaled $9.16.

"Thanks, Father," I said under my breath, "You never promised riches."

"Oh, this is for you, too," the preacher called as he walked outside with me. "One man had to leave early before we took the offering so he left this envelope with your name on it."

I mumbled thanks, stuck the envelope in my pocket and headed for the car. As we drove away, I steered with one hand and with the other ripped the envelope open.

Inside was a personal check for $100.

We had many lessons to learn about God's provision and about our attitudes in receiving that provision.

4

Ready—Almost!

The twelve months before we left the States were difficult. One day everything looked promising; the next clouds loomed black and ominous. Openings to speak came more frequently. I had traveled all through Iowa, and had meetings lined up in Illinois and Missouri. Offerings remained small and most of the preaching engagements were in churches of less than one hundred people.

Then, in November of 1960 events came to a climax. I fished a letter from Carlton Spencer out of the mailbox. It read:

> Due to the political unrest in Kenya itself, as well as the turmoil from the uprising in Congo, I suggest you delay your plans for departure. Our

> missionaries in Kenya are now on emergency notice to be ready to evacuate at any time.

He filled in further details. When Congo obtained independence on June 30, 1960, initial reports that filtered out were optimistic. Then, abruptly, came a chaotic political overthrow. Even East Africa felt the reverberations. Tensions mounted. People feared an uprising similar to the Mau Mau rebellion of the mid-1950s. Rumors hinted that uncooperative whites would be deported or killed. In the streets Africans shouted angrily, *"Uhuru!"* (Independence!)

Yet, missionary activities flourished. Upcountry, in isolated sections of Nyanza province, missionaries vaguely mentioned escape routes or means of survival. Yet they made little practical preparation because they had more opportunities for ministry than they could handle. One said later, "We couldn't really believe rebellion would come to Kenya."

As I heard rumors and exaggerated reports, I grew perplexed.

"Lord, I can't go on like this," I cried. "I don't know from one day to the next what's happening. Am I going to Africa or not? One day I'm certain, and then . . . a letter like this, and I'm confused and mixed up."

I asked God for a sign or a promise—anything that would assure me of His will.

"Lord, if I vacillate here, what will I do when things get bad in Kenya? I can't pack up and run home. I need assurance that will end my doubt once and for all."

That night I had a dream. Arthur Dodzweit and I sat at a table across from each other. As we conversed, I noticed electric lights and modern furniture. Centered on the handsome dark grained table was a bowl of peaches.

"I'm so glad you've come to Kenya," Arthur said huskily.

When I awoke in the morning I remembered the dream. As far as I was concerned, God had answered. From that moment on, I never doubted God's will about Africa.

I wrote Carlton and thanked him for his concern, adding one terse sentence: "We're going to Kenya: Elim or no Elim."

That dream stayed with me during the six years of missionary service in East Africa. It was one of the things that enabled us to endure the tests which followed.

By spring of 1961 we had cleared out our apartment and disposed of our furniture, including the children's toys. We packed extra clothes, dishes and other items in four metal barrels. We rented a four-by-six U-Haul trailer and headed east to New York.

Two months earlier we had made our last trip to Iowa to say good-bye to my parents. Neither of them was well, and both were in their late sixties. I faced the prospect that I might never see them alive again. The last day I tried to imprint everything in my mind—the house itself, my parents, the large garden Dad planted every year. A hundred things, yet all part of the composite picture of my boyhood home.

Leaving our home in Zion was even harder. For the past six years we had shared a duplex with Shirley's mother. We had grown extremely close. In fact, I looked upon Mom Brackett more as a friend than a mother-in-law. Shirley used to tease me when we were dating, "Did you come to see me or my mother?"

Cornelia Brackett could never express strong feelings of warmth, although she felt them. Anger and frankness surfaced during her conversations; but warm feelings struggled to emerge. However, she and I didn't need words for our relationship; we were kindred spirits.

On a crisp April morning we finished packing our brown 1956 Plymouth. The children had been excited all morning. Eighteen-month-old John Mark sang contentedly in his car seat. Wandalyn and C-C ran around the car, playing games and asking over and over, "Is it time to leave?"

Finally it was. Mom Brackett stood on the front porch hugging a coat around her shoulders. She waved to us and for the first time in my years of knowing her, I saw tears roll down her cheeks.

I wanted to hug her or say something to ease the pain, but somehow I couldn't. Mom understood. With a long look at each other, we parted.

I can still see her standing on that porch—tall, graying, regal and yet awfully proud that we were going to Africa.

As we drove down the street toward the highway, Shirley began to weep. Wandalyn kissed her on the cheek. "Don't cry, Mommy, Jesus will help you."

Shirley brushed the tears away and hugged her. "I know, but I'm going to miss Mom so much."

We had preaching services lined up in Indiana and Ohio. These helped with gasoline expenses as well as enabled us to present the need for foreign missions. Most of the churches had small congregations, usually less than fifty people.

Leaving Cleveland we faced a steep hill. The Plymouth had already put on nearly 100,000 miles, needed a tune-up and valve job. We crawled up the hill, but about a hundred feet from the top, the car sputtered and died. I started to back down, hoping to search for an alternate route.

After about fifty feet the trailer jackknifed on the winding road. We got out, wondering what to do next. Going forward was impossible. And I didn't know how to straighten the trailer, which already tilted toward the deep gorge off to the side.

"I could flag down a car to take me to a garage and hire a wrecker," I volunteered without enthusiasm.

Shirley didn't say anything; she was fighting back the

tears. The children played in the car, occasionally yelling, "Why are you stopping here, Daddy?"

Shirley walked to the rear of the car and looked off into the distance, still silent. I knew she was praying for guidance. The girls crept out of the Plymouth and began to play alongside the road. I took fussy John Mark out of the car and put him on the ground near the girls, making sure his coat was buttoned tight.

Then I went back to the front of the car, leaned on the fender, and silently abused myself for my stupidity.

"Honey, I'd better go to the top of the hill and slow down any oncoming traffic," I said, anxious to do something. A strange feeling came over me, I found myself running up the hill away from the car.

A blue pickup truck roared up behind me. Our Plymouth protruded two or three feet onto the road. The pickup swerved to the left to pass our car. I heard the truck but I had rounded a curve in the road and could not see it.

A gray Cadillac swooped over the crest of the hill at high speed. The pickup, unaware of the oncoming Cadillac, moved to the middle of the road.

A squeal of brakes.

The sound of impact and then a second crash, like crunching metal.

Too late.

The pickup had hit the left front fender of the Cadillac, and then ricocheted into our Plymouth, hitting exactly where I had been standing only seconds before! Then dead silence.

My feelings vacillated between horror and praise. Horror at what had happened: three damaged cars. But joy that God had spared our lives.

We exchanged names, insurance companies and essential information. Both men were able to drive away, but the owner of the pickup promised to send a wrecker for us. Twenty minutes later it came and pulled us out.

The collision had not only battered the left fender, but dented the grill, twisted the fan and punctured innumerable small holes in the radiator. How would we ever reach New York state? We carried little cash. Only that morning Shirley had mailed most of the money not needed for daily expenses to the bank. I opened my wallet and counted its contents. Less than twenty-five dollars. Shirley had three singles and a few pennies.

The mechanic, balding and friendly, shook his head as he examined the damage. "Well, I can work on it sometime this week."

My face paled. "Is there—is there any way you can do enough to get us on our way?" I asked. "It's important for us to reach Rochester tonight."

I didn't want to tell him we had no money to stay over.

He scratched his head and looked at the damage as though seeing it for the first time. He carefully pried open the hood.

Shirley then explained we were missionary candidates on our way to our headquarters. Finally she blurted out, "Besides, we just don't have enough money to stay over and wait until you repair the car."

The man scratched his neck, then looked at us silently for what seemed like a long time. "Well, I c'n bump out the fender so's it won't rub against the tire. Prob'ly straighten out the blades of the fan. Belt's a mite worn but you c'n drive 'er without much trouble. Only temp'rary but ought'ta get you there."

He stroked his chin and went on. "I've got some Stopleak to plug up the radiator. You'll need more anti-freeze 'cuz that's all leaked out, but we c'n plug 'er up. I'll give you a rope to tie the hood down. Won't look nice and ever'time you add oil or check yer batt'ry you'll have to untie it, but you c'n get on your way."

Within an hour we headed out of Ohio. The mechanic

charged only ten dollars for towing, labor, and antifreeze. Our simple thanks seemed so inadequate.

The temperature dropped steadily that afternoon. As we crossed the northern corner of Pennsylvania, snow flurries pirouetted before the windshield. The children, after all the excitement earlier, now settled down in the back seat. The radiator kept losing a trickle as we drove along. I had to stop and add water every hour.

Darkness had dropped like a curtain by the time we reached the New York Thruway. I sighed as I pulled toward the entrance ramp. "When we get this far, I feel like we're nearly there, even though it's still 200 miles."

But we never got on the Thruway.

Snow had accumulated. As we approached the entrance we saw a sign allowing no cars with trailers. We made a U-turn and took U.S. 5 and 20. This route was far slower with many hills and innumerable small towns.

After midnight we pulled into Elim headquarters, exhausted. People poured out of the building. One man took over the wheel and drove the car away after three or four others had quickly unloaded both the car and trailer.

"We'll drain the radiator for you, store it inside, and then we'll get it started again in the morning."

What a day!

"Do you suppose Africa could be this bad?" Shirley asked wearily.

I put my arm around her. "Honey, I'm too tired to think about it."

5

The Last $500

An extremely busy summer followed. We visited churches in the East from Ohio to Vermont and back to New York state. Meetings were arranged in Albany where we spent a week, then to the mountains of Pennsylvania and from there to eastern Ohio. By July we were worn out.

We drove the Plymouth with the rope tying down the hood. The fan thumped a little, but never gave any serious trouble. I had the radiator taken out, soldered and put back in. It looked awful, but the car never over-heated again.

But we had no way of knowing how long it would hold up. Each morning as I inserted the ignition key, we'd pray, "Lord, just hold this car together and keep it running until we reach New York City."

New York City! The place of our departure!

I did not have collision insurance myself but I made a claim anyway to the Traveler's Insurance Company—the company with which the owner of the Cadillac was insured. I wrote a letter explaining the fault was clearly his. I enclosed three estimates ranging from $212.43 to $359.

July highlights the year for our mission because that is the time of their annual convention. Our plan had been to attend the convention, then leave immediately after for New York City, where friends had scheduled a week of meetings. At the end of the week we would depart for Kenya.

Only one obstacle stood in the way: we still needed $500 to reach the minimum $5,000. Surely the money would come, for $4,500 had already come in. We were anxious to reach the field and begin work.

After diligent prayer weeks earlier, we had made the reservations for our flight to Kenya, feeling the money would be ready when we were. Everything had worked so well.

We prayed but nothing happened. No urgent calls to preach; no check for $500 handed to us by special delivery. The travel agent wanted at least half of the money by July 15.

"Lord, do we send in the money for the tickets or do we delay our flight?" We prayed and waited for an answer but nothing came. As I picked up the Bible it opened at the end of Isaiah. A verse I had underlined years before caught my attention: " . . . before they call, I will answer; and while they are still speaking, I will hear" (Isaiah 65:24).

The word of the Lord! We would leave as planned. I rushed over to the Elim office and asked the secretary to send in the partial payment.

Another secretary called me over to her desk. "By the way, we received an odd letter this morning from a woman in Mississippi who used to be your neighbor in Zion. She sent ninety dollars. The letter instructs us that if you leave within a period of six months from the date of this letter, we are to give you the money, but if you don't go within that time period, the money is to be refunded."

"Thanks for telling me," I said grinning, "and you won't need to worry about sending it back!"

"Thanks, Lord, that's the first part," I whispered. "It's still Your move."

I checked the morning mail and picked up several letters. The first was a letter from Shirley's sister, Edith, who lived in New Mexico. She and her husband were having a difficult time financially so we had not expected any help from them. God surprised us a second time that morning. She had enclosed a check for $100 which they had put aside to send us off!

A second letter looked like an advertisement and I almost threw it away. The Traveler's Insurance Company. It had been so many months since the accident and my claim I had figured nothing would come of it. They enclosed a check for $212.43

I quickly added up the sum in my head. I thanked the Lord and then reminded Him, "Okay, Father, where is the last $97.57?"

When in Rochester, we worshiped in a small church called Philadelphia. The people had warmly accepted us and had given us offerings on two different occasions. They pledged a monthly offering to us when we reached Africa.

Individually, the people showered us with kindness. Articles of clothing, small gifts of a dollar, five dollars, a book—all evidence of love and fellowship. One member, a nurse named Lucille, found out I wore prescription shoes (my feet demand a 7½ EEE). She took me downtown in Rochester, had my feet measured, and presented me with two pairs of shoes. "Whenever you need more, you write and let me know and I'll send them. Will you do that?"

"No, Lucille," I replied, "but thanks. We promised the Lord not to tell our needs to anyone. He'll provide."

She looked crestfallen a moment. Then her wide face beamed. "Well, I'll just have to ask you." And every year for the next six years, Lucille sent me a pair of 7½ EEE shoes.

On the closing day of the convention we attended all the services. During the day we received the letters and the Lord's promise. All day long I expected the last money to fall into my hands. But nothing happened. We checked the afternoon mail. Still nothing.

I would meet with Carlton and representatives from the board the next morning to assure them of our financial solvency. But where would I get the last $100?

The last worship service concluded and I stood outside the auditorium a few minutes. I felt confused, wondering what to do. How could I go in the next morning and say, "Well, God provided all but the last $100"?

"Hey, there you are!" a pleasant baritone voice interrupted my musing. "I've been looking for you all evening."

I spun around. Dan, a member of the Philadelphia Church, had not been at church the evening of our farewell.

"I was afraid we'd missed saying good-bye," he went on. "We know it's about time for you to leave for Kenya. Here." He thrust something into my hand. "Our family loves you and so does everybody in our church." Dan gave me a quick hug and was gone.

I opened my hand. Five twenty dollar bills!

The next morning I met with Carlton and two others. "With what I have in cash, slightly over five thousand dollars." (I didn't tell them "slightly" meant less than three dollars.) "Besides, we have a week of meetings lined up in New York City after we leave here."

Carlton nodded. Then he asked the final question, the one I had hoped he wouldn't ask. "Do you have enough pledged support?"

"Oh, yes, we have plenty of promised support," I answered as casually as possible.

I had said we had plenty of promised support because I felt fully convinced God would supply. Shirley and I had the inner assurance that when we left for Africa and had enough money to make the trip and get settled, God would take care of our day-to-day needs.

"May I see the list I asked you to make up?" he said with a smile. I had learned that under Carlton's warmth and radiance, there was at rock bottom a strong will. If he said we must have $240 pledged each month, he meant exactly that.

"Sure." I took the list out of my pocket and gave it to him, averting my eyes.

On the list were eight small churches and a dozen individuals who had volunteered to help. Few of them stated specific amounts. The Philadelphia Church had promised monthly offerings and I had jotted down: $10-$20 estimated.

I silently prayed he'd not prolong this part.

He looked puzzled. "Cec, most of the names don't have amounts, and those that do, you've written 'estimated' after them."

"Carlton, I didn't press them for specific amounts. You expect us to go to Kenya on faith. Fine. We believe God has called and the five thousand dollars amply shows God's provision. We're ready to leave and I ask you not to hold us back."

He turned back to the list again and studied it carefully. He cleared his throat nervously, got up from his chair, and embraced Shirley and me. "I won't stop you. I'll even meet you in New York City and drive you to the airport."

At daylight the next morning we packed the old Plymouth, stashing suitcases, toys and children in the back seat.

"Just one more trip, Lord," I prayed as we got into the Plymouth and pulled out of the mission driveway. "Hold the car together until we get to New York."

We reached Bay Side just before the rush-hour traffic. As we neared the home where we planned to stay, we heard a shrill piercing noise.

"Ohhh, Daddy, that's awful!" Wandalyn put her hands over her ears.

"Must be an ambulance or police car," I said as I craned my neck to see. The noise intensified and we still saw no vehicle with a siren.

Shirley glanced at me and, as our eyes met, we began to laugh. I said, "Praise the Lord! Praise the Lord!"

"What is it, Daddy?" C-C asked as she snuggled her head on her mother's shoulder.

"That horrible siren you hear, girls, is our car. We are now speedily screaming to a halt—literally!" I laughed again. What a time for the transmission to give out!

The noise intensified, hurting our ears. We rolled up the windows. That helped a little, but the whining grew louder, shriller and more deafening. I glanced down at the gas guage and realized our tank was empty. The temperature gauge suddenly arrowed toward the danger zone; the car had overheated.

"Thanks, Lord, for holding the car together until we got to New York. You really answered our prayer literally!"

The next day we sold the 1956 Plymouth for junk. They gave us twenty-five dollars.

6

Missionaries—at Last!

"Passes? This one—that's the only one Mr. Dodzweit sent."

I handed her the official-looking paper, signed and stamped in Kenya, made out in my name. She stared at the paper and then glanced up. "But . . . but you need others. I mean, for your family. Surely, you have a permit for your wife. You see, there's no mention of a family on this permit."

I gulped. "I didn't know. That's all I have. What should we do?"

The thin Englishwoman across the counter hesitated, tapping her lips with long fingers. "Take this to the British Visa Office at Rockefeller Center. Act as though you don't know any better and see what happens. It's right in Manhattan." She wrote down the address for me.

"Thanks," I said as Shirley, the three children and I headed out of the travel agency. "Don't worry, Honey, nothing is going to trip us up now. The Lord didn't bring us this far to have it foul up at this point."

I felt real peace in my heart, knowing it would work out. Forty-five minutes later we walked into the Visa office, handed our papers to the distinguished-looking man at a desk.

He went slowly through the tickets, the passports, and then glanced up at me. I kept my face as noncommittal as possible.

"This—" he held up the employment pass and asked in a clipped accent, "is all you have?"

"Is there something more I need?" I asked evenly.

He glanced back at the pass. "Have—have you similar passes for your family?"

"Why, no, I don't. That's all I ever received." My throat felt tight and I prayed, *Lord, please, please . . .*

"Hmmm," he mumbled. "Excuse me." He abruptly left his desk and disappeared into a side office.

Minutes later he returned. "You see, Mr. Murphey, the difficulty is that this employment pass," which he held up for me to inspect as though I had never seen it before, "covers only yourself. It says nothing about your wife and children."

"Oh," I replied, not knowing what else to say. I hated to admit how naive I was.

"We have decided to take a chance and let you go through. If we stamp your passports, I hardly think you'll be turned away in Nairobi. We shall try anyway." He stamped each passport.

On a warm, cloudy Saturday morning our plane swooped down at Entebbe Airport outside Nairobi, Kenya's capital. From the observation tower, we saw Arthur and May waving frantically.

"The Dodzweits!" squealed Wandalyn and C-C.

We're here at last, I kept saying to myself. *We made it. Now . . . let's see what happens at Immigration.* But nothing could dampen my exuberance.

To the Asian official I handed our passports and other important documents, trying not to look nervous. Carefully he studied the passports, thumbed through each of them, glanced at my work permit, and nodded.

"Welcome to Kenya, suh."

I grinned at him. "Thank you very much."

He saluted briefly and waved the next person forward.

After clearing customs without trouble, the Dodzweits drove us to their house in the city. Chatting and trying to see everything at the same time wasn't easy. We craned our necks, pointed, commented. Hundreds of times the girls asked, "What's that?"

Modern Nairobi puzzled and impressed us. We had expected primitive surroundings, with beating drums and wild animals skulking everywhere, much like the Tarzan books I had read during my teen years. Nairobi was fully in the twentieth century.

Five miles outside the town, as we learned a few days later on our way upcountry, time seemed to move backwards to a previous era. Simple mud and thatch huts, rocky dirt roads and dust-covered almost naked children herding cattle materialized suddenly.

Girls of six or seven toted tiny siblings, papoose-fashion on their backs, while tending grazing cattle. Gaunt women plodded down the dusty path, bent beneath the loads of firewood strapped across their shrunken shoulders. Yet everywhere we were greeted with smiles.

On our first day in Nairobi, Arthur had planned an evening meeting at a prison camp where former Mau Mau suspects were incarcerated. Many had responded to the preaching and teaching, and appeared eager to hear more.

Although we had not slept adequately on the trip, the excitement of being in Africa primed me for action. The children were bedded down by midafternoon and slept straight through until the following morning. We had lost eight hours in crossing.

"Honey, do you want to go to the camp?" I asked Shirley.

"Of course," she answered matter-of-factly. "I'd like to go along and play the accordion. She looked tired from loss of sleep.

"We'll see how you feel later," I said, knowing how determined she could be.

Shirley agreed to a short nap before the service. When Arthur and I got ready to leave, Shirley was sleeping peacefully.

After the service Arthur, May, and I sat and chatted. There was so much news to catch up on. May finally gave up and went to bed.

Just before midnight Arthur yawned, and then I realized for the first time I was sleepy. Arthur smiled at me across the table. "I'm so glad you came to Kenya."

The shock of his statement hit me. I glanced around: *It was the same room I had seen in my dream.* I stared at the modern furniture, the dark-grained table. Even the basket of fruit and electric lights! Not peaches as I had supposed, but filled with reddish-gold mangoes which I had never seen before. I had discounted the dream being literal because my concept of Africa had been only mud huts and kerosene lamps. I realized God had privileged me to peek briefly into the future.

As I undressed for bed I prayed, "Lord, I didn't have any doubts after You gave me that dream. Now I'm even more convinced You planned it all!"

I would need all the assurance I could find in the troublesome months ahead, especially during the first year. I had much to learn.

The next morning I got up, shaved, washed and dressed, and then awakened Shirley.

"Come on, time to get up!"

She opened her eyes slowly, frowned and asked, "Is it time to leave for the camp *already?*"

I roared with laughter. "Shirley, you have just slept sixteen straight hours!"

Her eyes popped open as she saw daylight streaming into the room. We both laughed.

Among my duties, I learned, I would supervise churches and evangelists of the Luo tribe, take care of a mission station, and become the "upcountry" bookkeeper for Suna Mission and the education department.

I discovered that "upcountry" actually did not mean geographical direction—at least in the case of Suna Mission which was nearly three thousand miles lower than Nairobi. Upcountry meant anything north and west of Nairobi, and especially Nyanza province, the more backward area of Kenya. We learned also to call it the "bush." Vegetation in this largely semi-arid country struggled to reach even the height of a few feet. Tall trees were rare.

On Wednesday Benjamin Maisori visited the Dodzweits. One of the earliest converts, he had been appointed to the Kenya legislature by the British colonial government. In addition, the missionaries themselves had selected Maisori to take over the education department from Tom Shattles, the man I was to replace at Suna.

A large heavy-set man, Maisori seemed friendly. I had already learned that fat Africans were still somewhat rare in Kenya. Maisori wore glasses, and had an extremely wide face, with the ear lobes cut off. I judged his age about thirty-five.

"If you want to stay here in Nairobi two more days," he

said pleasantly, "I can drive you to Suna Mission myself, or if you have a car by then, you can follow me."

I thanked him, but added, "I really need to get to Suna. The Shattles are anxious for Shirley to start taking over dormitory responsibilities. Besides, I want to take a look at the books."

It was a long time before I realized the importance of that last sentence. *Only later would I realize that the conflict with Maisori began with those words.*

7
Adjustments

On the first Monday in August 1961 I registered at various government offices. Afterwards, Arthur and I looked for a car. I didn't buy because my money had been delayed. My mission had supposedly mailed a check to Arthur two weeks before so he could look for a car while awaiting our arrival. No money came.

Monday evening Arthur telegraphed Elim:

> MURPHEY FAMILY ARRIVED BUT NO MONEY
> SO NO CAR. SEND IMMEDIATELY.

We checked the mailbox every day but nothing came from Elim. Arthur decided on Tuesday he would drive us upcountry in his Volkswagen. Over six feet tall, he pushed the front seat as far back as possible, leaving little room in the rear. I scrunched into the other front seat, while Shirley, Wandalyn, C-C, and John Mark squeezed sardine-fashion into the back. That still left our four suitcases, typewriter, accordion, two briefcases, and two satchels. He borrowed a luggage rack and somehow we squeezed everything in.

The streets of Nairobi were paved, except in the settlement projects. For the next fifty miles I craned my neck, marveling at the beauties of the land. The paved road curved sharply around the escarpment and we saw the famous Rift Valley for the first time. Following English law, Arthur drove on the left side of the road. He seemed to fly around the never-ending curves.

After nearly an hour I pointed. "Look at those narrow paths over there. What are they for? Driving cattle to market or something?"

Arthur laughed so loud and long that I felt silly. "Cec, you're looking at the road we'll be traveling on for the next seven hours!" he said finally.

"But—those look like winding cowpaths . . ."

"Yes, and besides all that, they're just barely wide enough for two cars to pass each other!"

At my startled look Arthur burst into gales of laughter. "Within a couple of weeks you'll get so used to these roads you won't think anything about them."

After nine hours of driving, we covered 300 miles, stopping only for gas and a quick meal. We reached Suna Mission just before midnight, exhausted, soaked with sweat, and grimy from the sifting dust. Only a few stretches of road had been paved in 1961, and it was too hot, even after the sun went down, to roll up windows. We preferred dirt to asphyxiation.

As Arthur finally pulled into the rambling driveway leading to the main house, I had to strain my eyes . . . there was only a sliver of moon that night. I finally made out a dim light in the window of the house. As we got closer I saw a kerosene lamp shining through a barred window, but nothing else. Before the car stopped, Tom and Liz Shattles ran out to meet us. The noise of any vehicle, we were to learn, can be heard for at least a mile before it can be seen. They had expected us earlier, but this was Africa. They knew we'd get there eventually.

Tall and graying, Tom extended a long arm for a friendly handshake. Liz, an attractive blonde, smiled as she talked. Their two young children were in bed.

In preparation for our coming, two mattresses had been placed on the floor in a third bedroom, and we gratefully sank down. Arthur drove on to Bukuria Mission—another hour of travel—to sleep, because the Shattles had run out of mattresses.

The next morning we met "Auntie" Princic, Henry Nyakwana, the overseer, and an endless number of local residents.

"Liz, how do you tell the Africans apart? They all look alike," Shirley commented.

Liz laughed. "You're just not past the cultural shock. Once you know them, you'll discover that black faces aren't the same. You'll soon appreciate the differences and learn to recognize African beauty."

Within the next two years, she learned, as most of us did, to look at an African's color and, with a high degree of accuracy, tell his tribe.

In Kenya, missionaries had pioneered almost all education, organized the schools, built classrooms and trained teachers. Gradually the government assumed responsibility. By the time we arrived in the country, government funds paid all teachers of properly registered schools.

Our mission continued organizing new schools in primitive areas, paying teachers a monthly sum from foreign funds. As these schools grew and met government qualifications, they were put on the federal budget. However, the missionaries still managed the schools and supervised the teachers.

Tom's job entailed a vast amount of travel, wisdom and patience. It was not easy to make decisions about schools. We had funds for perhaps ten or twelve schools, and requests to start at least three times that many. That was only in Kenya, and voices from Tanganyika were pleading for help.

Maisori replaced Tom—a landmark in 1961 because, so far as I know, he became the first African appointed to such a responsible position. It was the beginning of the era which we later called Africanization.

The first morning at Suna I awoke with light streaming in the window. I glanced at my watch—6:05. The sun blazed in shades of orange as it began a slow ascent into the heavens. The grass, still brown and scorched from the dry season, looked like a tan-and-mauve tapestry. Outside the window a fragrant pink flower (later identified as frangipani) lifted its delicate face to the sun.

"Africa, my Africa!" I said aloud as I opened the window wide and breathed deeply of the warm morning air. Birds sang softly in the distance, and clear and flute-like, girls from the dormitory were singing sadly. We later learned that all Luo songs were in a minor key—even when they were supposed to be in a major key.

"Thanks, Lord, for bringing me here. I know this will be the best and most wonderful period of my life!" I prayed.

A bus lumbered noisily down the road and paused momentarily in front of Suna Mission. Someone got on, and it grunted on its way. Moments later whiffs of diesel-laden air drifted up to my window.

After an American-type breakfast we explored our new home. We had naturally expected dirt floors, grass roof, and wild animals, but found, instead, a metal roof and a cement floor. The top layer of the floor was cement mixed with red ochre, which gave it a lovely sheen when waxed. The foundation was made of large stones and rocks with mortar in between. The walls were brick.

Shattles explained how Eva Butler, who had supervised the building of the house, had, in order to save money, used mud between the bricks instead of cement. On the outside, cement was used for pointing, giving an attractive touch to the house.

In addition to a small but adequate apartment upstairs where Auntie Princic lived, the house had three bedrooms, a kitchen, and a bathroom with flush toilet and pipes for running water. But the bathroom was used only during the rainy season; otherwise we used the little house at the end of a path. For bathing in the dry season, we hauled large barrels of river water.

A stone reservoir had been built under the house at the back door, with pipes leading upstairs to a fifty-gallon storage tank. Each day a worker hand-pumped the water, which we used exclusively in the kitchen, except during the wet season when water became plentiful. The house had been wired for electricity, but there was no current.

The Shattles sold us their beautiful furniture for $400—a wonderful bargain for us. Made by Hindus, it had been fitted together without nails. The wood resembled ash. There was a large, gate-leg table, a matching sideboard, two chests of drawers, and a bed in the master bedroom, all of the same wood. An American-made Simmons bed and mattress was in another bedroom.

In the master bedroom one chest of drawers spanned nearly six feet. It had four larger drawers on either side and six small drawers in the middle. *Two years later that huge chest of drawers was to save our lives.* An old-fashioned wood cookstove and a Swedish-made kerosene refrigerator completed the furnishings.

The refrigerator operated efficiently, taking only two days to make one tray of ice cubes in the freezer compartment. But it *was* a refrigerator! The woodstove worked well (could much go wrong?), except that the flue leaked and it refused to stop smoking. Occasionally, fumes filled the kitchen.

Since Suna is located in a semi-arid part of Kenya, wood was scarce. In order to use a woodstove we had to pay a workman one shilling a day (about 14¢) to get a load of wood. He left the mission with a wheelbarrow and axe, collecting broken limbs as he went along.

Our first grocery order, which came from Kisumu, cost us nearly one hundred dollars. After that, we learned to subsist largely on local products. Meat, which sold cheaply at the local market, was tough but edible. We purchased cornmeal, flour, lemons, oranges, bananas, fresh and dried fish, tomatoes, onions, cabbage, beans and rice.

The house at Suna soon became home. We had a fireplace which we used three or four times a year. Late July and August are the winter months for that part of the world. A few chilly evenings justified a fire. Once a thoughtful American friend sent us a package of marshmallows, which we toasted before the fireplace.

One by one we met the local people. Henry Nyakwana, a quiet, unassuming man, won me by his first words. He had a warm and sincere smile, and he spoke English well.

"We have waited and prayed for your coming a long time. For many months we have asked God to send a missionary to the Luo people. You are our missionary," he told me warmly.

Henry helped more in the days and months ahead than anyone else. As long as we remained in Nyanza province, he stood by me as friend and confidant, adviser and co-worker.

Nashon, who worked on the mission, spoke fluent English and seemed different from the other workmen. People who worked on the mission came as unskilled laborers, hired to collect firewood, cut grass with long-handled scythes, or to do simple and menial labor. A typical Luo with six bottom teeth extracted at puberty, and a wide round face, Nashon stood tall. Like most Africans used to heavy physical labor, I noticed the rippling muscles in his otherwise wiry frame.

"Yes, I do work here for the missionaries. It is because the Shattles have helped me. God saved me through their words and I do not wish to return to Nairobi where I worked as a clerk," he said graciously.

He told me his story one day. He had two wives, one of whom was sickly and the other a demanding harridan. Nashon could figure well, type, and had a quick mind. Then he began to drink and eventually lost his job. Soon after, the sickly wife died and the other tormented him all the time.

He continued, "One night I lay on my mat trying vainly to sleep. I had no friends left, for everyone avoided me. My wife now feared me because I beat her often with a stick. Many times she would run into the bushes and hide until I fell asleep. My children screamed when they saw me coming. Everyone feared or hated me and I was troubled. Many times I had decided to change, but I never did.

"Finally, I slept and had a dream. I saw no one but a voice spoke and said, 'Go to Suna Mission where they will tell you about God. If you stay here, you will die.' The next morning I called my wife and children and told them what had happened.

"When I reached Suna Mission I went directly to the missionaries and told them of the dream. They talked to me a long time and explained about God. They prayed with me and I felt a calmness in my heart. The anger disappeared and I found myself crying. Then I pleaded, 'Please allow me to work for you here at this mission. If I stay here, I can learn much about God and help others.'

"I have been working here at the mission since then. It is only five miles to my home and when I reach there in the evening, my children now come and play with me and talk to me. My wife has also changed. This God of the missionary is a good God!"

As I walked around Suna Mission the first few days, orienting myself to the country, Africans crossing the mission grounds called greetings to me. Africans consider it rude to pass someone without acknowledging their presence and asking of their health. The word for good morning is a tongue twister and to say it right took weeks of practice. *Oyare* is spelled easily enough, but its pronunciation demands four syllables and a slide.

There was one word I knew they'd understand. When they called to me, I'd wave and yell back, "Hallelujah!" This word seems never to be translated into another language, but only transliterated. The Africans, I soon learned, dropped the initial *h*. So for the first week when anyone greeted me I responded with "Aleluyah!"

They'd smile and rattle on in Luo.

When the speaker paused, I'd smile as broadly as possible and repeat, "Aleluyah!"

Somehow they must have figured that I was either a total imbecile or that I didn't know the language.

Shirley learned the language quickly. She began teaching simple Sunday School lessons within three months and I preached my initial sermon after six. Eventually we learned to speak fluently in two languages and could make simple conversation in two others.

Later I learned that because of my initial response of "Aleluyah," the Africans gave me a nickname. The Luo people, and most East African tribes as well, observe closely the customs, practices, and attitudes of white people, and name them accordingly. The names often show deep insight.

My first nickname was "Aleluyah." Later, they gave me a second name. I move rapidly, talk fast, and do everything in doubletime. My wife has complained over the years, "Cec, while I'm still thinking about doing something, you've already finished it."

They called me "Araka." This is a perverted form of the Swahili word which means "fast" or "quick." For at least the first year, everyone called me Araka, though I didn't know enough of the language to realize what they were saying.

Later, they added a third name which really pleased me. They called me "Omore" (O-more-A). A rough English translation is, "a person with a happy face." Shirley received a name which meant a person proficient in anything she tries.

8

Suna, My Suna

Occasionally we had white visitors. Some came out of curiosity. There was Bertha, for one.

Bertha's dark eyes swept across the desk, taking in every detail. She saw Shirley surrounded by bookkeeping accounts, records for the dormitory—including columns showing amounts of potatoes, corn meal, peanuts and tomatoes purchased that school term. She observed the stack of correspondence marked variously, "Dormitory," "Mission," and the opened file called "Monthly Reports." Pushed to the back corner of the desk were a dozen letters with a band around them marked, "Personal letters to be answered."

Bertha had come to survey the mission field for herself. For many years she had wanted to be a missionary.

"Frankly, Shirley," she said firmly, "if I had to get involved in keeping books, writing letters, and making balance sheets, I wouldn't be a missionary."

Shirley drummed her fingers on a memo pad. "Then, Bertha, you won't ever be a missionary."

That was Bertha's first lesson in what a missionary does. Two weeks later she said, "I'm glad I made this visit. Now I know I couldn't do it. I just don't have the physical and mental stamina to be a missionary."

Bertha smiled, but we knew that honest remark had cost her something. Her glamorous dreams of missionary life had been smashed. Unconsciously she had expected a life of going from village to village, proclaiming Jesus Christ. She envisioned heathen falling down and weeping, "Lord, save me!"

We quickly learned that preaching and teaching—and preparing for those messages—form only a portion of a missionary's time. Life was never dull at Suna. We kept books and made out monthly reports and wrote letters home. But we also did a lot more, as this portion of a letter I wrote to Shirley's sister shows.

> Last night we began supper about six-thirty and at least four people interrupted me so that I didn't finish the last bites until after eight o'clock. First, there was Kaleb. I recently led him to the Lord and he is so hungry to know more about Jesus Christ. I spent almost an hour listening to his problems and teaching him from the Word.
>
> After that, Joseph came . . . . Joseph is a good Christian brother, but extremely weak. He's one of those who must be talked to often and guided step by step. Our conversation was interrupted by a schoolboy who had been bitten by a dog. He came running up to the house, screaming and

pleading for medicine so he wouldn't die. The boy had only a small scratch so I put Noxzema across the injury and generously covered his leg with bandages, beginning at the ankle and up to the thigh. He thanked me profusely for such good care!

Joseph left, and girls from the dormitory came up complaining that they could not get their pressure lamps lit, so I had to help them.

After supper I sat down to fill out forms for permission to start a new church in an area where we've never been able to get in. By the time I had finished, Henry came over to help me with my Luo lesson—which lasted almost an hour. We are reading the Gospel of John each night, and it takes so long to get through a chapter because my vocabulary is still so limited. But Henry patiently works with me . . . .

This morning I spent time talking to a man who has been employed as a mason here. He is erecting a permanent building to add to our dormitory complex. He's not a Christian and the stories that circulate about him are pretty wild, but he's the best mason around and charges the most reasonable rates. Several times I've talked with him about the Lord but he just shrugs.

This morning, however, he came to the mission early and waited outside my door until I came out. After greeting me he asked, "How can I live a holy life? For years I've been troubled by *pombe* (a strong native beer) which has caused me to do many wicked things. Now I want to serve this God that you and the happy people at the mission sing and talk about."

. . . . Shirley is now teaching her daily Bible class

> at the school. She also teaches one on Thursday evenings in the dormitory. On Friday afternoon both of us go to Migori Asian School where we teach a full hour of Bible to those Indian children.

As mission stations go, Suna deserves some kind of rating for its smallness. One house for missionary staff, one permanent house for the African overseer, a girls' dormitory consisting of one permanent building for sleeping, a permanent kitchen, and one mud and thatch building. In addition we had a pastor's house of mud and thatch and six more just like it for the school teachers. The church differed from the houses only in that it was approximately seven feet longer.

That was Suna, but I loved it. Even during times of intense loneliness, walking across the mission nearly always revived my spirits. I would touch the gorgeous orange-colored blossoms of the Nandi flame trees, or smell the strange, tropical flowers. Or I would pause at the cacophony of golden crested cranes. Other times a stillness enveloped the entire community, and I'd have to strain to hear movement or sound of any kind.

Eunice Princic's cheerfulness quickly endeared her to us. She seldom complained. Short, slightly stout, she had a sallow complexion—because of continued use of quinine substitutes over the years to prevent malaria. Her twinkling blue eyes belied the tired-looking skin. She combed her hair in finger waves on the side and knotted in back, covered with a hairnet, a style of the 1920s. "Auntie" (as we all called her) had a loud laugh that carried completely across the mission station. Africans frequently lapsed into peals of laughter when she enjoyed a joke. Then she slapped her leg and chuckled even louder.

Because of that raucous, infectious laugh, the Africans

named her appropriately, "Adebe Jaraha," which means "a loud, happy noise." As long as she remained at Suna, everyone—Luo, Asian, Kuria, or Maragoli—called her by that name.

I remarked to Shirley once: "Auntie never learned Luo, and not much Swahili. But she and the Africans seem to communicate heart-to-heart and laugh-to-laugh!"

On Sundays she usually went to village churches with us, most of them a great distance from the mission. When the children were not at boarding school, all five of us climbed into the VW, followed by Auntie carrying a guitar that had to stand upright because of its length (and that meant it took up the equivalent of one passenger seat). We stowed Shirley's accordion in the space under the hood.

The first six months, Henry or one of the English-speaking Africans, interpreted. As I grew more fluent in the language, Henry and I could split up and he went to other churches.

What would I have done without Henry in those days? He taught us almost everything. When other missionaries appeared to turn their backs on us and a lot of the nationals with them, Henry remained constant.

Through Henry I learned my first lessons of love and compassion in Kenya. By living among us in love, Henry showed me the error of much of the advice I had received. First we had heard, "Never give an African anything free. Make him work for it so he will appreciate it more."

Through Henry I saw what it meant to care about the needs of people. He thought nothing of giving away his last shilling to someone in greater need than himself. When I asked him about this once he said, "Brother, when I feel someone's need, I pray. If the Lord directs me to give, then I give and I let the Lord worry about my needs."

I remembered the words of the Lord Jesus, "Freely you received, freely give" (Matthew 10:8).

A second word of advice was hurled at us often: "You must show the Africans you mean business. Don't let them get away with anything." That was one admonition I didn't need. Extremely willful and quick-tempered, I often battled to control myself. It was easy for me to assert authority, to make demands, to expect submission because I was the missionary. My own nature and the well-meant advice, I see now, caused my harsh attitude that led to the beating by the African teacher, Efraim.

A third piece of advice came from a senior missionary. "Africans are like little children. Treat them that way and you'll never have to worry. Preach like you would talk to grade-school Sunday School classes and you'll do all right."

One day it became clear to me that if the disciples preached the Gospel—even the deep mysteries of the faith—to uneducated people, who were we to teach simple evangelistic passages exclusively? Wasn't it our responsibility to proclaim the whole Bible? Paul, in leaving Ephesus after three years, said, "I am innocent of the blood of all men. For I did not shrink from declaring to you the whole purpose of God" (Acts 20:26-27).

Through the contributions of American friends, we presented Henry with a motorcycle so he could get into more inaccessible areas. He traveled often. A few times he and I bumped over the countryside together on his *pikipiki.* He was anxious for me to see how people lived in the remote villages; I was equally anxious to go.

Our first jaunt came after I had been at Suna only a few weeks. When Henry came to pick me up, I had a small airflight bag. He looked at me strangely and asked, "This is what you take?"

"Yes," I answered uncertainly. "Is—is it too much?" I had included my shaving equipment, Bible, notebook, and one change of clothes.

"No," he smiled, "that's good." He nodded and his eyes twinkled. "Good, brother, that is good."

How can I describe Henry's smile? His whole face went into motion, and even his eyes shone. (Many times later I was to see those same expressive eyes burn with anger. And once toward me.)

Henry's hair was cut so close above his round face that he looked almost bald. (African barbers cut hair with a razor blade held in the hand.) Like all good Luos, his six bottom front teeth had been extracted at puberty. Well over six feet tall, broad shouldered, he had the deep ebony shine of the Luo tribe. Luos originated in the Sudan area and came south more than a century earlier. They are the blackest of the Africans. Not chocolate, nor as light as most American Negroes.

Henry and I arrived three hours later at the church. It stood on a small hillside overlooking Lake Victoria. A soft breeze caressed my face and I could smell fish drying in the sun. In the distance fishermen worked from small sailboats on the lake.

It was an arid region. The people grew little besides cassava, a root plant similar to the potato, which they grind into flour. Cassava and the abundant lake fish provide the staples of the Luo diet.

During our stay I ate African food and drank the dirty, stagnant-smelling water. It took courage to gulp it down. Every time they offered me water straight from the lake with no purifying and no boiling, I prayed silently, *Lord, in Mark's Gospel You promised that if Your disciples drink any deadly thing, it won't hurt them. I believe that promise.*

In six years of service, only once did I get sick from African food. That was three months before I left the country. On that single occasion I had stayed three days in an area where the water was carefully boiled and food prepared as hygienically as possible. But, in order to show me great honor, the cook used some hints she had picked up from

Asians. The food was excessively greasy and pungent with spices. Within an hour I was deathly ill, retching and vomiting for hours!

Here on this trip with Henry when mealtime came, I ate the food as fast as I could shovel it into my mouth. Preachers, I noticed, nudged each other, and chuckled as they saw me eating without stopping. What they didn't know was that I was *afraid* of the food, and I was trying not to offend the Africans. Halfway through the meal I realized what was happening but could not seem to slow down.

At the end of the meal Henry commented, "You eat like an African! You will do well with our people and find acceptance with us."

I did not have the heart to tell him the truth.

We had three preaching/teaching services that day. In two services I taught and Henry interpreted. When I finished, Henry stood up and preached his own sermon—beginning where I had finished. I felt great warmth in those meetings. The preachers joked with me and those who spoke some English chatted incessantly between services. I knew so little Luo, but I think I used every word I knew and learned dozens of new ones.

When I made obvious mistakes in grammar, instead of laughing, they smiled and said, "Ah, you are serious about learning Luo. Keep trying."

The daytime meetings were designed to help the preachers become more effective ministers. But local people sat in on the meetings as well. During the evening services we encouraged everyone to come. Henry preached some stirring messages (at least, I believed they were from what I could figure out with my limited grasp of the language). When he gave in invitation each night, people responded.

That first night, tired from the bumping-thumping trip, two teaching services, continuously straining to speak in a foreign language, interspersed with large doses of African food shoved in front of me every time I sat down, I was ready to collapse for the night.

Henry led me to one of the houses. For himself, he had brought along an army surplus cot. I discovered that in my ignorance, I had brought nothing to sleep on. The Africans admired me for my willingness to live on their level, and gave me the only bed in the entire village.

I looked at the bed. *How can I sleep on that?* I thought. Then I smiled and thanked my host—determined I'd sleep. The bed was approximately four feet long and nearly three feet wide. I'm five feet eight, and there was no way to get comfortable in that bed. No mattress and no springs. Beneath me for padding, the owner placed a blanket over stretched strips of cowhide woven in rows across the width of the bed. A wooden frame made the bed a kind of hammock.

I curled, with knees drawn up in front. I'm one of those people who stretches the full length of the bed, so I tried lying at an angle. I propped myself up, half-sitting. Using my clothes for a pillow, I got back to my original stance of lying on my side in the fetal position. It seemed hours later that I drifted off to sleep.

Thus went my first safari with Henry. Hundreds more followed in the years ahead and I came to look forward to them. During those courses and conventions I made real strides in learning the language and the customs. Most of all, I experienced what it means to be loved and accepted by people who are not my own race.

9

Dormitory Troubles

"It's a thankless job," Liz Shattles had said. That statement proved an apt description of the work at the girls' dormitory. The boarding school brought us headaches and heartaches.

We were always strangers. Our white skins set us apart. No matter how much we attempted to think black or be black, there was always a barrier. We loved the girls, and we led some of them to Jesus Christ. But during times of tension, we learned that even our love did not transcend the color bar. And I'm sure that bar existed on both sides.

Then it was ingrained in their culture that no African ever opposed another African among outsiders. When white missionaries entered the picture, the Africans presented a picture of solidarity. I could not help but respect that. The

Africans had a great sense of community, of belonging to each other.

Over the years, however, we saw gradual changes. The day came when some of the Africans stood on the side of the whites and opposed Africans on the other side. But that day was a long time in coming—not until early 1967, just before we returned to America.

In 1961 eighty boarding girls lived in the dormitory. Kenyans had become conscious of the changing world and their part in it. All over the country the cry went out for better educational facilities and more educated young people. Many parents sent their daughters to school.

We provided housing, food, and supervision for the girls. We tried to enforce a rigid moral code. Even so, we lost several girls each year through pregnancy, some of them because of clandestine meetings with teachers; others because they did not always go straight home when the school term ended. We escorted the girls to the bus but could not go with each one to be sure she reached her destination.

We found no way to please parents, students, and teachers. At times we felt battered from all sides.

Among the girls, we had good times and bad. A girl would appear spiritually hungry, ready to commit her life to Jesus Christ, and then the end of term would come. Often they transferred to another school or didn't return due to lack of funds. But many did return. And we rejoiced to see professions of faith and evidence of real Christian growth. I recall Damar with the fiery temper, who submitted to Jesus Christ. Or Dena with the beautiful eyes and flawless complexion. Or a favorite, Jile, whose face glowed when she talked.

Angelina came to Suna because our boarding fees were cheaper than those of the Roman Catholic mission where she would have preferred to go. A strict Catholic, she found our ways difficult at first, but by the end of 1962 I wrote home about her:

> God has changed Angelina and filled her with the Holy Spirit. She is now a strong leader among the other girls. It is such a joy to watch her lead singing and joyful praise to the Lord. This term her younger sister, Helen, transferred to our school and only recently made a profession of faith.

One of the girls, Rose Aje, was a poor student and seldom seemed to care about anything (quite unusual because the students were keen on education). No matter how hard we worked with her, Rose Aje only rebelled. Then God met Rose and she changed as completely as any person I ever saw. She became a top student and, even more, a real spiritual leader. She began teaching Sunday School and developed into quite a preacher. And because of the great change in her life, when Rose Aje exhorted, the others listened!

One evening near the end of term, Angelina and Rose Aje asked for permission to sing a special duet. They chose (in Luo), "I gave my life for thee, what hast thou given for me?" As they sang, Rose stopped in the middle of the first verse, unable to continue. As Angelina carried on, Rose listened as though she had not heard the words before. Rose dropped to her knees and began weeping. Then Angelina also began to cry. Within minutes a praise service had turned into a prayer meeting! Both girls dedicated their lives to the Lord that evening. And their later actions showed they meant that decision.

Missionary organizations set up their first schools to train

Africans to read the Bible. Until independence, most of the schools in remote areas were still operated by missions. Around 1960 the government began paying teachers' salaries but left the schools under mission control. This often created tension—especially when the governmental agency was not interested in the religious aspects of school life.

First came the trouble with Efraim, the beating he and the school boys gave me. For days afterward, the thought nagged at me, *I've failed. Lord, I've let You down.*

I stayed in bed for nearly three days. Not that I was weak; I was discouraged.

"Here I take a stand for righteousness and end up beaten for it," I grumbled.

Henry Nyakwana visited me. So did several pastors. Occasionally local Christians came to offer sympathy. Or to stare. I was not sure which.

"God, is this what You brought me to Africa for?" Again I grouched.

I had upheld the standards. That gave me a certain amount of satisfaction. At least initially. The Scriptures promised that the godly will suffer persecution, which put me in company with the great disciples of the faith.

Or . . . or did it . . . .?

I didn't want to pursue that line of thinking. *Of course* I had done the right thing. Efraim knew the rules, and he deliberately flaunted his authority.

But nagging thoughts occasionally surfaced. Had I handled Efraim right? Had I talked to him in *love*?

I could not resolve that question then. I was not able to admit any blame.

For two weeks I read my Bible and prayed almost feverishly. *Give me directions, Lord. What do I do next?* But the heavens seemed brass.

I can't turn around and go back to America. The Lord had led me here. I would stay until He sent me home.

During that period other missionaries may have offered friendship and love, but *I felt* only rejection in their presence. As though they judged me because of the beating. As though they blamed me for Efraim's continued breaking of dormitory rules.

I found one marvelous source of comfort. A plaque hung on our bedroom wall.

> And we know that all things work together for good to them that love God, to them who are the called according to His purpose.
>
> Romans 8:28.

All things. Strange words.

"Lord, even if I'm wrong in my attitude, I know You're at work in my life. Somehow You'll use this experience and other experiences to mold me into the kind of missionary You want," I conceded.

Peace.

Three years would pass before we heard from Efraim again. *That,* we thought, *was the end of our troubles.* But, it was only the beginning. The teacher replacing Efraim was a Luo named Musa. Dark, handsome, Musa walked like a man expecting respect. He was a KT-1, the most educated teacher we had ever had at Suna Mission.

Troubles started with Musa, just as they had with Efraim. The difference was strategy. Musa was subtly defiant. He never directly disobeyed a rule. He smiled; he pleaded ignorance. He kept the girls only twenty minutes late. ("We were working on some problems, and I knew you wouldn't mind if I held them for a few minutes. After all, education is more important than many duties at the dormitory.") Things like that.

The climax came in late January when Musa instructed the girls to spend the entire Saturday at school. They had dormitory duties which included washing their uniforms, their mattress covers, and cleaning the entire dormitory compound. We refused to allow the girls to go to school, offering no explanation.

The following Monday morning he punished them for not coming to the classroom by making them crawl on the fine gravel in front of the school building until blood oozed from their lacerated knees.

Auntie Princic saw what was happening when she went down to teach her class and rushed back to inform me. I was furious.

Thrusting a bicycle toward one of the workmen, I shouted: "Hurry out to Migori and get the education officer. And make it snappy!"

Inwardly I seethed. The more I thought of the girls' brutal treatment the more my anger boiled.

Each teacher at Suna Mission had been provided a house. Only one of them had a cement floor; two had metal roofs. The rest had mud walls and grass roofs. Each teacher was to take care of his plot of ground, keep the grass down, and keep it swept clean. We had only a few rules: no corn planting on the mission property. Corn breeds mosquitoes and Suna was a high malaria area. In fact, the word *suna* is Luo for mosquito.

Musa had planted corn on the mission earlier in the year, and I had forced him to pull it up. He resented it, although he smiled even then. He replanted the corn five feet behind the mission line where I could do nothing about it. Whenever I walked past his house and saw the corn, my irritation mounted. But Musa only smiled.

He also made a circular driveway in front of his house so that friends with cars could turn around easily. He had planted flowers along the edges, all without permission. Not that I minded the flowers, but I always suspected that he did these things in defiance of the rule which stated that anything of this type had to have approval.

That morning as I saw the bleeding knees and girls sobbing on the ground outside the classroom, my anger reached its limit. Impulsively I rushed to Musa's house and banged on the door. There was no answer.

The teacher's wife in the next house opened the window and yelled out in Luo, "The headmaster left for a trip a few minutes ago. He has gone to see the district education officer in Homa Bay."

Angered and frustrated, I stood there, shaking. Then I saw the flowers he had planted. I stooped over and ruthlessly pulled up every single one of them, flung them in front of his door, and stalked back to my house. At least I felt better.

But I had many things to learn. My actions triggered the wrath of the local people. They did not stop to ask the reason; they merely said, "That is the way white people behave. They destroy. They tear up." So far as I know, none of them bothered to look at the bleeding knees or listen to the sobbing cries of eighty school girls. A teacher always has the right to punish however he wishes.

The other teachers also showed hostility. One of them said mockingly one day when I disagreed with him, "If I speak up, do you destroy my flowers too?"

We felt alone in a black world. My temper had alienated us.

Nor did I get any encouragement from fellow missionaries. Of course I was wrong—I knew that three minutes after uprooting the flowers.

One of the city missionaries said, "You'll never win the Africans now, Cec. No matter how long you remain in Kenya, you'll never minister effectively again."

"I worked for years to build good relationships with the

Africans," a woman missionary said. "I feel as though all our efforts have gone down the drain."

My heart sank. I was being very "Araka" (quick-moving) again. Would I ever learn?

Another missionary put his arm around my shoulder and said, "I'm glad you're sticking it out. I never believe in running away when you've fouled up. Perhaps the Lord will give you a chance to redeem yourself."

Someone else said, "Cec, you've got an awful temper."

"I know about my temper. I'm trying. But—but I can't control it," I admitted.

"But God can! However He has to control you first."

I knew she meant those words lovingly, but I could not hear them that way. There was too much pain inside.

I felt even more alone.

Next to the beating I had sustained two months earlier, this became the lowest point. I needed a helping hand. Encouragement. Friendship. There was none—at least not any outward manifestation from my white colleagues. Except for Eunice Princic. Henry understood and several African Christians encouraged me. But their voices were so few. I was alone, an outcast among my fellow missionaries.

"Lord, please, please let me return to America. I've ruined everything," I cried. It seemed I was always calling the shots to the Lord.

At that low point Romans 8:37 flashed into my mind. I knew God had spoken. "In all these things, we overwhelmingly conquer through Him who loved us."

I didn't feel like a conqueror.

I didn't feel much of anything.

Except alone.

I loved the land and the people. I knew the Lord had sent me. And yet . . . yet everything had gone wrong. All my glorious missionary visions smashed.

"Father, why did You send me here? With my awful temper, why did You let me come and ruin everything?" The agony ground into my spirit.

Yet, even in that lonely evening, I never questioned that God *had* sent me. That assurance helped.

"I don't understand . . . but I'm staying. I'm going to do the best I can for You, Lord Jesus."

As I brushed away the tears I also reminded Him, "It hurts so much to stand alone."

But I was learning that God has not promised that co-workers, friends or blood brothers will sustain us in our times of despair or loneliness. He does promise, "*I* will never desert you, nor will I ever forsake you" (Hebrews 13:5).

10
Opposition

By late February 1962, the beating and the flower episode began to recede into the background. Education authorities reprimanded Musa, transferred him to an isolated school, and demoted him to the position of junior teacher rather than headmaster.

Our troubles should have been over, but we were learning that trouble never ends. This was only a mild calm before the next storm.

That storm arrived in the person of Benjamin Maisori. It had started, I found out years afterwards, when I commented, "I want to get upcountry and look at the *books*." My statement meant that Tom Shattles would be leaving shortly and I wanted to make certain I could figure out how to do them. In high school I had taken one semester of bookkeeping and while I remembered the fundamentals, I had serious doubts about keeping several sets of books.

But to Maisori my words meant I intended to usurp his position as manager of our schools. He had reason to be suspicious. For years mission societies had made promises they had not kept. Talk had been floating around that Africans must make their own decisions, but in actual practice, the missions gave the orders.

By the end of 1961 Africans were assuming positions of responsibility in government and business. Our mission had no precedent for Africanization, but our small size enabled us to start the wheels moving quickly. I think Maisori's basic fear was that he would have title without authority.

From the beginning he watched me warily. But I saw him only as a man who had taken an instant dislike to me.

Then the matter of the mail convinced Maisori his suspicions were right. After Tom Shattles left, mail continued arriving addressed to him. I had no way of knowing whether it belonged to Suna Mission, to Tom personally, or had to do with educational matters. Simple enough, I decided. I opened each letter, read enough to grasp the nature of it, and if it pertained to education, I passed it on to Maisori. He never said anything when I explained what I had done.

Months later he accused me in front of several missionary and African leaders, "And he reads my letters! I don't even know if I'm getting all of them. Is he afraid to allow me to open my own mail? Can not an African be trusted?"

My mail opening had continued only three or four weeks, but in his mind, it had gone on indefinitely.

Even though we had differences, I respected Maisori as an unusually gifted man. A member of the Kuria tribe, one of the more primitive of those in Nyanza province, he had lived all his life near Bukuria Mission. This small tribe is wedged in between the Luo and Masai—both enemies of long standing.

The story goes that Maisori showed up at Bukuria Mission one day wearing nothing but a simple blanket—the normal amount of clothes for that tribe and for that period of time. He asked for work.

Young Maisori had ear lobes stretched to his shoulders. Blocks of wood had been inserted between the lobe and the ear itself at the time of puberty. Yearly, larger blocks were inserted to stretch the lobe lower and lower. After he grew to manhood and had been educated, he had the lobes surgically removed.

The Sicklers hired him to work for them in their kitchen at Bukuria. Maisori proved quick to learn. One evening, Bud Sickler found Maisori sitting in the kitchen holding a Swahili Bible under a dimly burning lamp. The boy, totally absorbed in himself, did not hear the missionary enter. He was hunched over, sounding out words, a letter at a time.

Maisori was teaching himself to read. He would hear the Bible read in church and then go back to the missionary's house and try to read it for himself. Sickler was so impressed that he took Maisori under his care and saw that he received schooling. Maisori studied at school, then worked two or three hours in the evening to pay for tuition, clothes and food.

Upon reaching manhood, he began to preach in the Kuria area, traveling around as an evangelist. Gifted with words, he quickly emerged as a leader among the Kuria people. He was instrumental in starting several churches. Later, Sickler helped him attend Bible school in north Nyanza. At Bible school his teachers had the highest praise for him. One instructor remarked, "His mind absorbs like cotton. He takes in everything you teach."

Maisori became the second African ordained by our mission. In 1960 when the British set up a provisional government in Kenya, the white governor appointed

Maisori to represent the Kuria tribe in the Legislative Council. When independence came in 1963, Maisori won the post of minister (like our senator).

Maisori and I seemed unable to work together, although we both tried. Late in 1962 he came to Suna Mission and called a meeting of the local people to discuss the school. We did not know any Swahili or enough Luo to follow what went on, so we didn't attend. We heard later.

Maisori denounced me as one who would destroy the educational plan for the Luo people. He urged the local people to insist that I be sent back to America.

"This man has now run off two headmasters—both excellent, qualified men," he said vehemently. "How many more must this white face chase off before we get him out of here? He despises Africans! We do not need missionaries like that!"

Frequent rumors reached us of political and educational meetings in which Maisori denounced us personally, and missionaries in general. He said little of this openly to me, although to his credit, he never pretended friendship. I tried to break down the hostility, but on each occasion I felt rebuffed, so I gave up.

News traveled rapidly among the mission staff. Again I looked to my fellow missionaries for encouragement, but to no avail.

One woman who had been on the field four years said, "After all, we've known Maisori longer and we never had any trouble with him. We can only assume he's right in what he says."

She had spoken frankly; the others remained silent. Perhaps they remembered my displays of temper. I learned things about Maisori. If I told what I knew, people might think I was only out to degrade him. But to remain silent meant ignoring what I felt was misconduct. I chose silence.

I had no actual proof of misconduct, only vague rumors

at first. But then from reliable sources we learned Maisori had begun to drink. This carried more stigma among Africans than it would have in America.

But even more serious, he had secretly taken a second wife. Maisori was an ordained church leader. Paul's qualifications for church officers stipulate, "the husband of one wife" (1 Timothy 3:2). We felt this verse settled the question of polygamy, and Maisori knew the teaching well. If a man had more than one wife, we encouraged him to support his wives and live as an exemplary Christian, but we would not allow him to become a church leader.

Eventually, Maisori acknowledged his second wife and resigned from the mission. By then, several of the missionaries had begun to see him in a different light. Two missionaries made feeble attempts to tell us so, but their concern had come too late to help us.

I sometimes wonder if we could have helped Maisori if I had been more sensitive to the feelings of anger he was putting out. He and I really had similar problems; we only manifested them differently.

Daily, Luos passed our mission. Many of them, more concerned about education than the progress of the church, resented the poor teachers assigned to Suna.

We always felt Maisori purposely sent the least qualified teachers to Suna to spite us. We couldn't prove that and he always insisted, "No one wants to teach at Suna as long as you're there." (Which may have been true.)

Resentment from local tribes people grew. Sometimes when they passed the house, they yelled threats and even shook their fists. We began to wonder if our lives were in danger. Yet, somehow the Lord always gave peace and we could say, "We're here as long as Jesus Christ wants us to remain."

On February 13, 1963, Maisori called a meeting of the

Luos living in the Suna community. We were purposely not invited, although I could have insisted on attending. I had previously made plans to go to Kisii that day.

At noon I sat in a little *hoteli* (an Africanism for restaurant) having rice and tea. I had felt discouraged all that day, knowing Maisori would use the meeting to blast me again. As I started to eat, I took out my pocket-sized New Testament and it fell open. One sentence seemed to leap out at me: "And the natives showed us extraordinary kindness" (Acts 28:2).

A word from the Lord! My spirits lifted immediately. God would give us favor with the people. That day would come . . . surely it would come. And from that moment on, I never doubted its fulfillment.

When I returned at dusk, Suna lay blanketed by quietness. The sun had dipped behind the horizon, and the red-orange glow at the rim of the world faded into pink behind the distant mountain range. Even when I heard what had happened, I wasn't disturbed.

Maisori, I learned, had demanded our removal in more vehement terms than ever. Several Africans vocally agreed with him. But Blasio, the pastor at Suna, as well as several church members, stood up and argued with Maisori. So far as I know, these were the first words spoken in our defense in any meetings. Nothing came of Maisori's demands, and he never held any more meetings to denounce us.

From that time on, our relationship with the Luo tribe around Suna gradually improved. Many tests followed but we had passed the worst. The Lord was teaching us to trust Him, especially when I felt alone and in a situation that, with more experience, I could have handled better. My next big conflict occurred with a missionary. The trials ahead were of an entirely different nature.

11
Deception

Lee's dark eyes blazed as he said emphatically, "I don't want to have to carry you, once we get to the field!"

Too stunned to reply, I merely stared at him. I had never heard him talk like that before.

We had returned from a meeting where we had both spoken and were discussing our financial situations. He had had all his monthly support pledged for some time, but still lacked more than two thousand dollars to get to the field. I had just admitted our lack of monthly support.

All East Africa missionaries under Elim had agreed to help each other financially. If one received more than his allotted figure and another received less, the surplus would be given to the one lacking.

I vowed that I'd never take any funds from Lee's account,

no matter how poorly we fared. Ironically, twice during our years at Suna, the Nelson family fell short in their pledged support. Once the mission board cut us twenty-five dollars and another time thirty-five dollars, and the money went to the Nelsons. I wish my attitude had been kind about it, but I confess that I secretly enjoyed the humor of the situation.

The first real breach between us began over a simple matter: we reached Kenya first!

Largely, Lee depended upon the mission to make contacts for him. We, on the other hand, had made our own contacts and were able to leave in the late summer of 1961. The Nelsons arrived two months later.

We made the 600-mile trip to Nairobi to meet Lee, his wife, Helen, and their two children at the airport. We had written that we would be glad to help them go through customs, visit the necessary government offices, buy initial provisions, and then escort them upcountry.

The first remark Lee made after greeting me was startling: "So now I have to look up to you as a senior missionary because you beat us by six weeks." He was not smiling, his voice low and hard.

I laughed. "Six weeks doesn't sound like much seniority to me!"

"I hope you'll remember that then!" he growled.

"Lee, I hope you'll forget it!" I answered hotly.

Lee was an enigma to me. At one time he could be the most tender, most gentle person. Several times when he preached, tears would come to his eyes and I felt a deep emotional response. At other times, his chiseled features hardened, his motions stiffened and the black eyes grew cold. More than just moodiness, it was as though two distinct personalities struggled for mastery.

Almost from the start, Lee conflicted with everyone. His tone to the Africans sounded surly and abusive. Eventually they nicknamed him "Bwana Kwenda." I do not think he ever really understood Swahili. If an African wants someone to leave, he says, *"Ende."* That's the polite form of command. To animals in the field to get them moving an African shouts, *"Kwenda!"* To use *kwenda* in the imperative when referring to people suggests rudeness. It implies you think of that person as no better than an animal.

Lee never learned to speak Swahili, other than enough words and phrases to bargain with. The Africans, I'm told, actually introduced him as "Bwana Kwenda."

Shortly after Lee arrived upcountry, he went to Migori market with me. By then; I had learned enough to communicate in simple sentences. We walked across a large open compound. Africans sat on the ground under the broiling sun, displaying tomatoes, dried fish, citrus fruits, and bananas. A group of women showed baskets they had woven. Another group of men proudly displayed simple cloth-wick lamps they had designed.

I helped Lee purchase fruit and then we went to the "meat market," the only permanent block building. Each morning the butcher slaughtered a cow, skinned it and hung it on a massive hook suspended from the ceiling. Flies buzzed in the small room and perched familiarly on the meat. No African asked for special cuts because they boil all their meat, regardless of which portion they get.

Lee wanted ten pounds of meat and I passed on the request in halting Luo to the Maragoli who ran the store. He stood with blood-soaked apron and a sharp sword, nodded that he understood, and whacked off several pieces, weighed them, and began wrapping the meat in newspaper.

"I don't want all that slime! Tell him to give me a decent cut that can be eaten!" Lee muttered darkly.

"Lee," I lowered my voice and tried to explain, "all meat has some fat on it. It's good meat. At a shilling a pound, you've still got a good bargain."

"If I want slime, I'll ask for slime!" he said adamantly, his chin jutting out.

The butcher, holding the parcel of meat, looked bewildered. He asked in Luo, "Did I give the wrong amount?"

"It is nothing you have done," I said.

The meat cutter shrugged his shoulders, laid the meat on the large chopping block and took another customer's order. Several Africans crowded around, their silent faces asking what was wrong. Lee kept up a monolog on how awful the meat looked.

"Did you tell him?" Lee asked angrily.

"No, I didn't. If you don't like the meat, you tell him. I don't know enough Luo to explain your rudeness!"

I smiled at the meat man, thanked him for waiting on us and left. Seconds later Lee carried the parcel in his hand as he came out of the building.

"I certainly won't go back there again!" he said as he caught up with me.

"Fine. He'll manage to get by without your business, and you'll manage to get along without meat, too!" I lashed at him.

I realize now that my angry retorts never helped Lee. Many times in the months afterwards I wondered what might have happened, had I been less volatile and more understanding. But I found myself erupting as quickly as he.

Lee and Helen Nelson went to Bukuria Mission where he supervised the station and churches among the Kuria tribe, the oldest but smallest work. Lee also supervised eight churches in Tanganyika.

Wallace Opunga, leader of the Tanganyika work, was the first and oldest African preacher in the mission. An easy-going, gentle man, he did not exercise the initiative and aggressive leadership so badly needed for the churches to leap ahead.

Lee worked hard and put in long hours. He had no sympathy for anyone who didn't push himself equally as hard. He quickly sensed that Opunga was not a pusher, nor a strong leader. In business meetings I attended where both men were present, Lee constantly accused him of shiftlessness.

I always felt that Lee lacked the same leadership qualities, but in a different way. Opunga allowed others to push him along; Lee attempted to force rather than to lead. Opunga spoke softly and often with humor, while Lee yelled harshly and demanded.

Lee dismissed one preacher, he told me with considerable satisfaction, because the evangelist could not account for an African five-cent piece recorded in the offering book. (This was less than one penny in American money.)

In the beginning, despite our differences, I liked Lee. Perhaps I pitied him, knowing his background. While still in his teens, he became an alcoholic. For at least three years he lived only for the bottle. After his remarkable conversion in his early twenties, Lee's life changed drastically. Though he could scarcely read, he felt strongly God's call on his life and applied for admittance to Bible school. Lee set an admirable record: he completed high school by correspondence, studied full time in Bible school, and worked enough to support his wife and two children.

Yet he always puzzled me. His desires seemed to be right; he had remarkable zeal for the Lord. But he could not get along with people. Lee never understood another person's weakness and yet seemed so blind to his own shortcomings.

Within two months after reaching Kenya, Lee and Wallace Opunga were hopelessly at odds. Lee could find nothing complimentary to say about the work in Tanganyika. He had been there only once; he did not know the language; and he did not understand the hardships of starting new churches in a sparsely populated area.

He kept saying, "Sand! Nothing but sand! That's what Opunga's work is built on! We pay him to supervise there and he produces nothing."

By the end of 1961 Bud Sickler, the missionary field secretary, called a meeting of upcountry missionaries and African leaders. In that meeting the brethren decided that because of irreconcilable differences between the two men, Tanganyika would come under my supervision.

I didn't ask for the added responsibility and hesitated to accept it. I knew this change would further antagonize Lee. But I was secretly pleased. Perhaps I was one step closer to being the successful missionary, and by comparison with Lee, my star shone brightly.

I shrugged my shoulders and said, "I'm here to work for the Lord. I'll do whatever you brethren think best."

From that time on, the friendship between Lee and myself—if there had ever been any true friendship—began to disintegrate. He left the meeting sullen, feeling everyone had ganged up on him. In a way, we had. I never spoke up once in his defense—although I could have said a few things to back him up in his evaluation of Opunga. But I realize now that I wasn't loving enough or sensitive enough to Lee's needs to speak up.

By the next day, Lee began secretly accusing me to the Kuria people of plotting to take over his work. He told them that I would become the missionary over all of south Nyanza province and would give the Luo people preferential treatment. I had schemed to make him look like a fool in the eyes of other missionaries, but God would vindicate!

Lee used another tactic which took me a long time to figure out. It was so subtle, I had no reason to suspect him. All I knew was that men from the Kuria and Maragoli tribes became cool toward me, and some of them showed outright dislike. By the time Lee's "campaign" got into full swing, the work at Suna was prospering and revival had started. We opened new churches every week in the Luo area and averaged one a month in Tanganyika. At the same time, the Kuria work suffered from apathy and internal dissension. Although they opened two or three new churches, they closed down as many old ones. I heard rumblings from some of the Luo preachers of Kuria dissatisfaction, but I tried to keep out of it.

I had become the bookkeeper for both mission stations. That meant I audited the Bukuria accounts. I had been asked to do this because neither Lee nor Helen could grasp accounting methods. Lee resented my doing the Bukuria books but he had no choice. Each time he brought me the accounts, he seemed more hostile.

I wonder now why I never saw the reason. I was becoming *the* upcountry missionary. He had lost part of his responsibility to me; I did the administrative work. Because I typed, the Africans elected me to do all the upcountry reports previously done by the Bukuria missionary.

Inside I felt secure and smug—even though I wouldn't have admitted it. I worked hard and results showed. I could always handle another job or an added responsibility.

One day Lee stopped by Suna on business. We had a good time together. He smiled and joked and seemed more relaxed than he had in months. He even asked my advice about planning a training course for pastors.

Just before leaving, Lee casually mentioned the African overseer at Bukuria, Joseph Muhingira. I had always thought of Muhingira as hard working and dedicated. In fact, I remarked once to Shirley that he must be a very patient man to put up with the resident missionary's harshness.

"Muhingira's a good man, but you have to watch him closely," Lee said, lowering his voice confidentially.

I had heard only high commendations of Muhingira, although he and I had never worked together. "That surprises me; I've always thought of him as dependable and trustworthy."

Lee bent forward and muttered, "He's out to grab every penny he can! Always begging for more money, always complaining about how hard it is to get enough food and clothes. He's lazy, too. I have to force him to get off the mission station and supervise the work. Otherwise, he'd just sit at home and do nothing."

"I'm sorry to hear that," I replied. "I'd never thought of Muhingira like that."

"Don't you think we ought to take action against him? I mean, don't you think we ought to start proceedings to remove him as overseer?"

Like the lamb ready for the slaughter, I said impulsively, "I sure do!"

Six months later at our annual meeting of all missionaries and nationals, Muhingira and I differed publicly over a trivial question. After the meeting recessed for the day, Muhingira marched up to me and lashed out, "You! I know your plan to get rid of me! You want me out of the Kuria area so you can put one of your Luo friends in charge!"

"What?" I could hardly believe I had heard correctly. "Why would I want to do anything like that?"

He stood rigidly straight, towering above me. "I know my friends! I know my friends!"

That statement puzzled me and I pushed him for more answers. At first he answered vaguely.

Finally he hissed, "Did you not speak against me to Brother Nelson? Did you not yourself, right at Suna Mission, right at your own house, tell Brother Nelson that I should be replaced?"

My face blanched. "Do you believe I would say a thing like that? Why, I wouldn't even suggest such an idea!"

"From the things I hear about you, I could believe anything!" he said and stomped away.

I didn't want to believe what had just happened . . . and yet . . . Muhingira could not have made up a wild story like that. I searched my memory for a long time before I recalled the incident with Lee that day. From that moment on, I carefully watched what I said to Lee.

As time went by, I discovered that Lee had taken many harmless statements out of context and blown them out of proportion. In a few instances, it appears he actually lied!

I made an attempt at reconciliation. "After all, Lee, we're here working for the same Lord, the same missionary fellowship, and the same purposes. Let's do it as friends."

"I've always tried to work with you!" he argued.

I prayed silently, *Lord, please don't let me fly off the handle now.*

"Okay, Lee, I'm not interested in blaming you. I am interested in unity."

"So am I."

We talked nearly an hour. Some of the difficulties, long hidden came to light. Lee did not actually acknowledge any wrong doing (and that was all right with me), but I felt he genuinely wanted peace between us.

We knelt and prayed together.

As I started to get up, I saw tears streaming down his cheeks. I dropped back down and prayed silently for him.

"God, God, forgive me," he moaned aloud.

Impulsively he hugged me and begged, "Forgive me, Cec. I've wronged you in a lot of ways."

"Sure, Lee, and forgive my failures, too."

We left each other with kind words and promises. I felt a genuine compassion for him. Our warm relationship lasted several weeks. Soon stories circulated again, and this time I quickly recognized that they had originated with Lee.

Finally I cried out in desperation, "Lord, I can't go on like this anymore. I have to leave this for You to solve. You never promised to give us an easy time. But I can't spend all my energies combating the stories that Lee spreads."

Again the Lord gave me peace.

The situation at Bukuria grew steadily worse. Several preachers left the ministry. Others made secret visits to Henry, pleading for something to be done.

The climax came one Sunday. Lee and Muhingira visited Rongo Church where the pastor had not submitted to Lee's demands. Lee insisted that each pastor fill out written forms each month, telling the number of villages visited, services conducted, conversions counted, and hours spent in counseling and witnessing.

The preacher at Rongo declined. "God knows my work. Let him judge it! If you have confidence in me, you need no reports. You don't fill out such reports for your mission board!"

Lee went to Rongo to explain to the people that he was dismissing the young pastor. "I'll send you a new preacher—a good man who will work faithfully and obediently for God."

An elder rose to his feet. "You have no right to speak like that. This pastor loves us and works hard. We have seen much fruit from his work."

Lee argued in English while Muhingira translated. The elder replied in Swahili and Muhingira interpreted into English. Lee refused to back down. He had set the standards and if a man wanted to preach for God, he had to obey.

"I cannot be faithful to Jesus Christ and accept any less," he snapped.

The church people became so enraged that they threatened to beat Lee physically.

Muhingira grabbed Lee's arm and pulled. "Let's go. If we stay, who knows what will happen to us?"

Lee's sense overcame his anger and both men hurried out of the church. The elders contacted our field secretary. Lee received strong reprimands and an uneasy feeling came upon all of us. What would erupt next in the Kuria area?

By 1964 it became obvious to everyone—white and black—that Lee would only further alienate and destroy. Rather than send him home, Africans and missionary leaders decided to give him a final chance. He moved to Jinja, Uganda. Within a year, he had nearly destroyed work which had taken another missionary four years of careful planning and praying to build. The field secretary requested the mission board at home to recall him.

When Lee left, I remember thinking how my impression of missionaries had changed. Before going to Africa I thought they were only two steps behind the archangels. Now I saw *us* as fallible human beings—like the rest of mankind.

A few weeks after Lee left, some of his actions came out more fully into the open. One missionary said to me, "When Lee used to visit, he told us all kinds of stories about you. I wonder why we ever believed him."

I felt hurt. Why had people believed without questioning, merely accepting anything he said? And yet . . . hadn't I done the same thing when Lee lied about Muhingira?

I still had many, many lessons to learn.

God has not promised skies always blue,
flower-strewn pathways all our lives through.
But God has promised . . . grace for the trials . . .

12
Robbers

Prowlers at eight o'clock on Sunday morning? It could not be. Yet as I watched, the stranger gazed intently into a window, moved a few feet, then shielding his eyes with his hand, peered into another window. While we had become accustomed to curious stares and undisguised curiosity, something about the man disturbed me.

He was not a Luo. His high-light coloring and facial structure looked Tanzanian.

I went out to see him. "*Jambo*! (Hello)," I called and then asked in Swahili, "Are you looking for someone?"

"Ahh, no, not for someone . . . " his voice broke off and he giggled. He had been standing straight and now he weaved backwards a few steps. Was he drunk? I smelled nothing (and the odor of native brew is potent!). I decided he had probably been smoking bhang, the dried leaves of the Indian hemp plant which produce a narcotic effect.

He looked neat, dressed in clean khaki shorts, a faded but clean blue shirt, and a pair of shoes. He carried a walking stick, cut from a limb but smooth. He leaned back on the stick so that it became a seat. Bending forward, he said in heavily accented English, "You have money at your mission. I know all about it. I know many secrets! Others know about this money and may attempt to steal it. Watch carefully, *msungu* (white man)."

He stood up straight, nodded to me, and then started to weave his way up the path toward the road. "Even tonight," he called over his shoulder and continued moving away.

The Tanzanian was right. I had nearly three thousand dollars in African shillings. On the previous Friday I had driven to Kisii to cash the monthly check which came from overseas to assist national preachers in starting churches. I brought the money home and hid it in a locked strong box in my closet. On Monday, the overseers planned to visit Suna. They would count out the money for each evangelist and put it into small, brown envelopes.

Shirley called me from inside the house. She had finished washing dishes and was dressing John Mark. The scheduled preaching service that morning was at a church three hours drive from Suna. I had no time to worry about the stranger's bluster. But I wasn't really concerned about robbery. Not at Suna!

After a long day which included a four-hour service in the afternoon, we prepared for bed. As usual, I lit the small kerosene lamp we kept burning in the hallway. Wandalyn had rheumatic fever and occasionally cried out in the night. The burning lamp enabled us to get into her room quickly without stumbling over everything.

As I drifted off to sleep I heard Auntie Princic's quiet movings upstairs. Crickets chirped a lullaby outside our bedroom windows in the darkness.

Snap! A noise aroused me instantly. I raised to a sitting position.

"What's that?"

Shirley sat up, cocking her head. "One of the kids must have dropped a toy from the bed again." Only the night before, John Mark had taken a top to bed with him. In the middle of the night it fell to the cement floor and awakened us.

"Yeah, I guess so," I agreed. I rolled over and settled back to sleep again.

Cra-a-a-k! That was the sound of a door being forced off its hinges.

I leaped from the bed and ran toward the side entrance. In the hallway I saw *them*. In the small lamp's eerie light, I counted six men. They carried hammers, swords and sticks.

I blurted out, "What—what do you want?"

The first one, and tallest of the group, rushed at me and yelled, "We want you—to kill you!"

I dashed back into our bedroom. "Shirley . . . wake up!" I screamed, my heart pounding.

She had already awakened and reached the door a split second after I got back inside. I slammed the door behind me and leaned against it. Together we struggled to hold the door closed. I screamed for help at the same time, but I knew no one could hear me.

That heavy six-foot-long dresser of the Shattles stood less than two feet from the door.

"Hold on, Honey," I cried and ran to the opposite end and shoved. I never thought about the weight—I just pushed. The dresser slid, barring the door. We leaned against the dresser, praying and yelling for help. What else could we do?

The large window on the west side of the room had heavy iron bars, installed to prevent petty thievery. No way out there. The other window, on the north side, was small and nearly five feet off the floor.

"Out the little window, Honey!" I told Shirley as the idea hit me. "I'll hold this as long as I can! See if you can slip out and run to one of the villages!"

Shirley grabbed a chair and climbed up to the window. As she yanked the curtain back, a large stone flew through the window, shattering the glass.

"Some of them are still outside!" she sobbed as she fell to the floor.

The Suna house had been well-constructed and properly insulated, and sounds did not carry outside. But when the stone shattered the window—immediately followed by a barrage of smaller stones—Shirley's screams were heard, one African reported, at least a mile away!

Ordinarily, Africans don't go out much after dark, but on this occasion, one of the school boys, Richard Ogada, unable to sleep, got up and strolled around outside the house he shared with a teacher.

Suddenly he heard Shirley's piercing screams from the other side of the mission.

Richard rushed toward our house and saw at least thirty men surrounding it.

"Oy-yo-yo-yo!" He let go with an ancient Luo war cry.

His repeated cries aroused others, and seconds later the answering "Oy-yo-yo-yo!" reverberated across the mission station.

Upstairs, Auntie awoke, peeped out the window and saw the men surrounding the house. She opened her window and shouted and prayed in English and her meager Swahili.

Someone yelled, "Kill that old woman!"

Footsteps pounded through the night as teachers, students, and neighbors rushed to our house. Others flung open their shuttered windows and gave the eerie war call: "Oy-yo-yo-yo!"

All the while the robbers beat relentlessly against the bedroom door. Bracing myself against the huge chest, I could feel each blow as it hit. What with the frenzied pounding, the thumping of my own heart, and my own prayers and shouts, I was oblivious to the pandemonium outside. A hammer broke through the wood and I saw the gleam of an angry eye against the splintered hole.

"White man!" a voice rasped. "Open up, and let us in. We won't hurt you. We want only your money!"

I didn't trust the robbers.

"Lord! Please . . . save us!" I screamed.

"Oh, dear God in heaven . . . help us . . ." Shirley's anguished cry rose above mine.

Suddenly the beating stopped, and we heard footsteps retreat and fade away. I didn't open the door. It might be a trick. We waited breathlessly.

We heard the sullen grinding of a truck engine starting, the growl of its shifting gears, and then it roared away into the night.

Relief flooded over me. I breathed: "Thank You . . . Oh, Lord, thank You . . . "

The children! Were they safe? We rushed to their rooms. They were fast asleep. They had slept through the whole turmoil, and didn't waken until the house milled with Migori police and curious neighbors later!

Again, I could only utter brokenly: "Thank You, Lord . . . thank You . . . "

Two nights later we heard that a Roman Catholic mission had been attacked the same night. The tiny mission served by only one priest, lay in a remote area more than a mile from the main road. The priest, an Austrian, had apparently fallen into a drunken stupor before the bandits attacked and wasn't aware of what was going on. He was badly beaten, his arms and legs mutilated with *pangas*—two-edged flat swords—like a machete. He lay in the Kisumi hospital nearly two months recuperating.

We did not know if the robbers would return. For nights

afterward the slightest noise awakened us. Many nights we had to pray for a long time before we could relax and go to sleep.

I tried a trick also which helped us rest easier. I kept a small kerosene lamp burning in the living room. It could be seen dimly from outside through the heavy curtains. In front of the lamp I placed a doll—an actual three-year-old sized doll a woman in New York had given to our girls. I propped the doll up in a sitting position. From outside, one got the impression someone was sitting up at night. Robbers preferred a surprise attack when everyone is asleep.

The district officer urged me to get a license and buy a gun. I agreed after much persuasion and obtained the permit, although I never felt right about buying a gun.

"God sent me to love, not to kill," I argued with another missionary.

"Yes," he countered, "but if it comes to them or my family, I'd kill them."

"You may be right, but I'd prefer to believe God would rescue me again!"

I never bought a gun and never felt the need of one.

But the incident gave me an idea, and I employed another trick to discourage future robbery attempts. In Nairobi I picked up a handful of firecrackers and a cap pistol. Evenings at Suna were generally quiet. Only sounds of distant drums from Giribe and the soft cadence of night insects throbbed in the darkness. One night I went to the front veranda and exploded a firecracker. I set off another, and then shot twice with my cap pistol.

Instantly doors flew open and heads poked out all over the mission. Voices yelled back and forth asking about the noise.

"It is nothing!" I yelled back in Luo. "I have a special *bunduki* (gun). I'm practicing with it. Don't be afraid!"

By morning I knew the word would spread everywhere about my *bunduki.* Some would even describe it and others would tell of my expert marksmanship. None of them knew I had not purchased a gun—I simply did not talk about it. It was well known that I had a gun permit. I wanted to make any would-be robbers hesitate. Even though I knew I could never kill anyone, it didn't bother me to create the illusion.

13

Faithful Friendship

Young Henry Nyakwana walked nearly fifty miles to Bukuria Mission because he wanted to learn to read and write. He chose Bukuria because he had heard they helped penniless boys pay the school fees. Coming from a family of eleven brothers, Henry was penniless.

The missionaries accepted Henry in the school and he studied eagerly. After completing the schooling, he became a teacher.

Henry had taught only a few months, when Arthur Dodzweit announced a teachers' refresher course at Bukuria. All Elim teachers were required to attend. Aside from offering help in teaching, Arthur preached once a day. On the second day of the course, Arthur preached from John 16.

"Those words warmed my heart and spoke to me. I knew that I had not come to Jesus Christ before, but I also knew that I was coming to Him then," Henry related afterwards.

When Henry returned to Giribe he had radically changed. He confronted all the students with the Gospel of Jesus Christ, and continually talked to the other two teachers of their need for salvation.

When the school term ended, Henry returned to his home in Karungu. During the month's hiatus he went from area to area, calling people together. Henry had only one sermon—the message which he had heard Arthur Dodzweit preach. He taught songs he had learned from the missionaries. Some of them, written only in Swahili, he translated into Luo so the people could understand.

Henry traveled all over Karungu Location, preaching the same message. Each time he issued an invitation for people to make a public commitment, as Arthur had done. In every instance people responded.

Before school started again he contacted Arthur Dodzweit. "I do not want to continue teaching. I wish to preach."

"You really don't know enough yet," Arthur answered. He was dubious of Henry's ability and perhaps reluctant to see a new convert launch out so quickly. "Right now we need teachers in the Luo area and that, too, is a ministry."

Henry returned to Giribe. Again he preached his sermon from John 16—still the only one he knew. Finally, the other teachers contacted the missionaries and begged them to get a different teacher in the school. "We have no teacher—he spends all day talking about God!"

Arthur visited Henry, explaining the grievances of the people. The missionary paused, watching Henry's face, waiting for a denial of the charge.

"No, they speak the truth, brother," he answered, smiling. "I plan to teach the students according to the books and I have many lessons worked out. But when they sit in front of me and I start talking to them, I can only tell about Jesus Christ. Without Jesus, life is nothing. I plan to teach or give an example and find myself preaching. No, they speak the truth to you."

Arthur gave Henry the opportunity to preach.

Henry went to Nyabisawa—which later became the site for Suna Mission. He started a church there, trained one of his converts to assume leadership, and moved on to a new place. By the time I reached Kenya in 1961, there were forty-one Luo churches. Henry had personally started twenty-seven of them!

But by 1961 a general malaise had settled over the Luo work. A lot of explanations could be given: poor missionary supervision, lack of personnel. In 1960 two missionary women from Canada had supervised the Suna work and had treated the preachers so badly, I heard, that several of them joined other denominations. Those who remained were discouraged.

Even during this difficult period Henry worked on. Filled with a zeal I've seldom seen in other men, he traveled constantly. He preached, counseled, opened up new churches, disciplined pastors under him, investigated grievances—and never complained about overwork. Whatever the need, when people called upon Henry, he was there—and he loved his people.

Henry became my close friend during those years at Suna. During that time we had only one falling out, which was actually my fault.

Each month all pastors and evangelists came to Suna in the afternoon, spent the night and left by noon the following day. We transacted business, gave reports, and shared experiences. Henry and I also used this as an opportunity to hold two or three training classes.

Nashon was one of those who came. He had worked at

Suna since the days of Tom and Liz Shattles. After months of menial labor, he felt called to preach. We sent Nashon to several short-term training courses.

Nashon opened a work about twelve miles from Suna and frequently stopped in to see me. I always enjoyed our talks, but the man bothered me. A quick-thinking, intelligent man, he seemed content living in the bush, making fifteen dollars a month. He could easily make a hundred in the city.

On his frequent visits to the mission, Nashon would mention a little rumor or gossip about another preacher in an off-hand way. After following it up, I found that in each case Nashon had spoken the truth. I thought his concern was for righteousness and I commended him.

At one monthly meeting of preachers, routine business went on which didn't require my presence so I returned to my house to type a few letters. Minutes later Nashon appeared at the door. He came in, we had a cup of tea, and talked a few minutes.

"I am surprised you are not attending this part of the meeting," Nashon said. He smiled, revealing large teeth with a wide space between the two center ones. Leaning forward, he added in a deep, gravelly voice, "It is about you that they are talking."

"Oh? What about?"

"Henry and three of the leaders have decided you are no longer needed. They want to run the work by themselves. Henry wishes to live in this house and chase you out. He will become the big man of all Nyanza."

I stared at Nashon. "But—but Henry and I are friends. He's never talked that way before!"

"Of course not, *Omore,*" he replied, calling me by my African name, "but it has been in his heart a long time. I heard them plotting with my own ears. Now they plan to get all the preachers behind them and write to the field secretary to send you home."

Betrayed! Shock waves surged through me. My mind clutched at fragments of previous conversations.

Older missionaries had warned me about Africans, "They appear friendly and become confidential. You trust them and find out later they've been planning to knife you in the back all along!"

I had argued. "People are people—there are good Africans and bad—just like whites!" But now . . . now I was no longer so sure.

"I am your friend, Omore," Nashon added, "and I will be with you. I beg you this much, please do not tell them that you heard this from me. Only watch!"

"Say nothing? Oh, no, we'll face this head on!" I flung out brashly.

Nashon argued, "It will do no good. They will only deny everything."

"I'll have to think about this, Nashon," I mumbled, "so please excuse me now." I walked into the bedroom and lay down. The news overwhelmed me. Henry—my friend and teacher. Henry, my companion and brother. It seemed hard to believe, and my mind spun.

Well, I'd put a crimp into that crazy idea in a hurry. No one made a fool out of Cec Murphey! I would be big and noble . . .

I swung out of bed and dashed off a quick note which I asked a workman to deliver. I wrote:

> Dear Henry,
>
> I have heard of the plotting you brethren are doing. If you wished me to leave Suna so you could have the house and become the single leader, all you had to do was tell me. If that is what you want, I'll write to the field secretary myself and ask for a transfer.

Minutes later Henry knocked at my door. He threw the note on the table and looked at me a long time without saying a word. I tried to read his face. Anger? Pain? I could not tell. Yet I had never seen Henry look that way.

Suddenly his eyes blazed and his words tumbled out, "He lied to you. I would never ask you to leave! You are my friend."

I stared at him, hardly able to grasp the words.

"I have known for a long time that Nashon whispers to you," he went on, "but I have said nothing. He wants my job as overseer. Every time he comes to the meetings he whispers against me to the preachers. He tried to convince them to support him as overseer." Henry's voice sounded cold and distant, so unlike the gentle Henry I had known.

Of course! It had never occurred to me to question Nashon. I had been so gullible.

"Henry . . . " I gulped, despair in my voice, "I'm—I'm wrong and I'm—I'm sorry. I only promise that if anyone ever comes to me with a story about you again, I'll not listen until you are face to face with that person, and there's proof."

We shook hands. His large, powerful grip nearly crushed my fingers. Then he hugged me.

Six months later my promise was put to the test. Before Lee Nelson's troubles removed him from the field, he casually remarked to me, "I've been hearing things about Henry . . . . that he's not totally honest in the way he handles money. I've heard that he pockets some of it on the side . . ."

"Wait a minute, Lee," I interrupted him, "I don't want to hear any more. If you have anything to say about Henry—even if it's only a rumor—don't tell me until I can call him over. Then you tell us both what you've heard."

"I—I can't prove it. I've just heard about it, that's all," he parried.

"Then forget it. If you have any proof—or you're willing to face Henry himself, then we'll talk about it. Otherwise, I don't want to hear another word against him."

Lee Nelson never talked to me against Henry again.

In late 1963 we obtained permission from the district officer to build a church in Migori, near the open-air market. Every Monday people traveled as much as forty miles to the market. From Lake Victoria they carried fresh and dried fish; from Kuria country they brought bananas, corn and tomatoes; from other parts of Luo country, they carried baskets on their heads loaded with onions, lemons, oranges, and pineapples. By noon Monday, three or four thousand people milled around the market place.

We mapped our strategy. Henry and his wife Margaret, Shirley, Auntie Princic, and I, along with two pastors, went to Migori and formed a circle under a eucalyptus tree. Shirley played her accordion and Auntie strummed the guitar. Within minutes some thirty eager Africans clustered around us, utterly fascinated, as we sang.

The crowd increased, pushing slightly. Henry broke out of the circle and stood in front of us. He preached a brief message on knowing Jesus Christ; then he stepped back into the circle and we started singing again: "Yes, God is good . . . yes, God is good . . . ."

A few church members joined our circle, adding volume to the singing. In Africa we never thought of singing a song through only once, even if the chorus consisted of only four short lines. Since there were few hymnbooks, and many of the songs were not even in the books, we repeated a song several times.

Other days of the week we visited market places in other locations and started open-air meetings. People always listened, joined in with the singing, and welcomed us back.

Many listened, but few committed themselves to Christ.

In 1956 an awakening began at the coastal province when Evangelist T. L. Osborn held a crusade. People testified of healing from deafness, blindness, and deliverance from demonic spirits. Churches sprang up as revival swept along the coast. We heard about it, but none of the revival fires had reached Suna.

"Henry," I said in early 1962, "we need an outpouring of the Holy Spirit. We've worked hard, putting ourselves as completely into this work as we know how and not much has happened. Let's start daily prayer meetings. It's the only thing we haven't tried."

"Good idea," Henry answered calmly, and he meant it.

The next morning we started the prayer meetings. Usually only six of us attended, sometimes as many as ten. We met in a small concrete building and knelt on damp, cold cement. We determined to pray every morning until God sent an awakening.

We prayed for the locations by name. "Lord, open the door for us to take the Gospel of Christ to Gwassi Location . . . to Kadem . . . Karachwonyo . . ."

We also determined that we would not force our way into an area. "Lord, we believe You will open doors," we said. "When people ask us to come and teach them about Jesus Christ, we will know You have made the way."

We prayed a week and saw no change.

Another week. A month. Two months . . .

14
Revival

By April 1962 both Henry and I realized God had begun answering our prayers for a spiritual awakening. During February and March attendance in worship services and open-air meetings grew slightly; we sensed stirrings of new interest here and there, but hadn't really thought of these as preludes to the moving of the Holy Spirit.

MacCalder Mines, located fifteen miles south of Suna Mission, produced gold and copper. For years our missionaries had attempted to get permission to start worship services there. The Mines provided housing, stores and schools for its workers, but no church.

In April the manager of the African housing complex sent word that we could use the local school building for worship services.

That church at MacCalder Mines became significant because workers came from all over Kenya to work in the mines. Some stayed a few months, others for years. As they returned to their homes they spread the message of Jesus Christ.

Later in April I called all the Luo pastors to come to the mission station for two weeks of training. Lee Nelson and all the Kuria pastors cooperated in this venture.

At the end of the first week during an evening meeting, a stranger walked in and sat down in the back. While we had designed the course for pastors and church workers, a few others attended. This tall, thin man sat hunched into a corner, absolutely silent. When we sang, he made no attempt to join in.

After the meeting the stranger approached me.

"My name is Jakobo Chuwodho (in English, Jacob Mud), and I have walked from my home in Karachwonyo to see you," he told me.

Henry gaped. Karachwonyo was seventy miles away! He had actually walked on foot the entire distance! We sat down and a few pastors gathered around us to listen.

"One of your school boys here at Suna, named Daniel Owino, comes from our village. Two weeks ago he came home for the holiday period. Each morning he has gone to every house, calling the people together, explaining to them about the good God you preach.

"I have been possessed by demon spirits for a long time. Most days I can work in my *shamba* (farm) only a short while, and then they attack me and I go wild. I beat anyone who approaches me, and often three or four people grab me to hold me down until the spell passes. Daniel saw me being restrained by men from our village and when I had calmed down, he prayed for me.

"Then the young man said, 'You can be delivered from these powers. If you go to Suna Mission, you can find help.'

"I have come this distance and you must help me. When

these evil powers come, I beat anyone around. One day I shall kill someone if I am not delivered."

His pleading gaze moved from face to face. He was a picture of hopelessness. His eyes, a dark brown that seemed black, moved without luster. His clothes, a khaki shirt and khaki shorts, were badly soiled, and his bare legs and feet were muddy. He looked emaciated.

Henry and Muhingira said, "We'll take charge of this. We'll feed him first and then pray with him. If it takes all night, we'll stay with him until God sets this man free!"

They prayed from eleven that night until nearly three the next morning.

When I reached the school to begin the devotional period at seven the next morning, Jakobo sat in the front row next to Henry. I stared. He smiled with large, gleaming white teeth. His eyes twinkled with pulsating excitement, and I thought, *He is one of the handsomest Luos I've ever seen!* Then I chuckled to myself. *Last night I thought of him as one of the ugliest!* I could hardly believe the contrast.

"Are you Jakobo who came here last night?" I asked, then felt foolish.

"Yes, but I am a new man today. I have found what I came for!" He gave me a wide grin. I couldn't keep from staring at him all during the devotional time.

Jakobo stayed at the training course two full days, absorbing every word. It made me realize how worthwhile it is to be a missionary.

On the third day he called Henry and me aside. "I must go back to our village now. You have helped me and I beg only one more thing: please come to our area and start a church!"

Henry's eyes met mine and I found it hard to restrain myself. This impassioned plea from Jakobo was an answer to prayer. *Karachwonyo was one of the locations for which we had prayed daily.*

Jakobo, not understanding the look, seemed adamant. "I refuse to leave until you promise to come! Please, just one time, and you will see many hungry people!"

"Brother," Henry answered, slapping Jakobo's shoulder, "You need not worry. We have prayed many months for God to open the door to Karachwonyo. Do you think we could refuse what God provides? Within a week we shall be there."

Five days later, Henry and four African pastors headed for Karachwonyo Location. They didn't come back that night, and I wondered what had happened.

Not until late in the afternoon of the second day, did they return. Henry's face told me what I wanted to know even before he greeted me.

"It was the most wonderful meeting in the world," he finally said. "When we arrived, the people had set up a brush arbor to protect us from the sun. People gathered at eight o'clock in the morning, although we didn't get there until noon. We counted 160 people waiting to hear our message.

"I preached, then Naftali preached, and Nathaniel after that. Then I stood up and preached again. We stopped to eat and said we would return to Suna. They refused to let us go. 'No, no!' they insisted, 'you must stay and preach more.' So we stayed and preached that night.

"The second day—this morning—I preached about Jesus healing the little girl who was left for dead. Someone interrupted and yelled, 'Can God heal today?'

" 'Of course. Is He not the same today as when He walked on earth?' "

As I got the report, an elderly man had stood up. "We have a woman here who cannot walk. Is your God strong enough to heal her?"

"Nothing is too hard for God," Henry replied boldly.

Three people carried in a woman, Rosali, on a crude pallet. "She fell down a mountainside when she was three years old and has never walked since," someone explained.

The five preachers stood together in front of the people. Each preacher laid hands on Rosali, prayed for her and waited. Henry knelt down and said in a commanding voice, "Get up and walk!"

Rosali stared at him but did not move.

"Did you not hear? Are you also deaf?"

She shook her head and mumbled, "No, I hear."

"Why do you wait? We have asked God to heal you. Get up! You are healed!"

Slowly she raised herself to a sitting position; then edged one leg to the side and finally touched the ground. She swung the other leg over cautiously, shifted her weight to her hands, then to her feet and slowly stood up.

"I—I *am* healed!" she screamed in Luo.

"Of course," Henry replied, "God does not lie!"

When the five preachers started to leave, people pleaded with them to stay. One elderly woman grabbed Henry's hand. With tears streaming down her face she wept, "You are leaving. Who will feed us? You are taking the Word of life away from us."

A wizened old man said, "You cannot leave us. You must teach us more!"

"We are leaving but we'll send a man to teach you," Henry told them.

Two weeks later, Isaka, a flaming young evangelist, moved to Karachwonyo and set an impressive record. At the end of six months the church had a membership of 250 people. Isaka worked with two young converts, taught them, and sent them out. They established churches eight miles in either direction.

Revival had come! God had answered prayer.

Nearly a year later, Gwassi Location opened to us. This especially was an encouragement to us because it was the last of the areas we had prayed for. People from Gwassi Location, after hearing about the Elim work, had visited the still new and struggling Kadem churches. Greatly impressed, they returned to Gwassi and shared the news with friends and relatives.

"Please come to Gwassi and start a church for us," the people begged.

"I will give a plot of ground for you to build your church on," several volunteered.

We had only one obstacle: the chief of the location.

A chief is an appointed official, similar to a mayor or sheriff. He is responsible for the over-all care of the location. This chief was a staunch Roman Catholic. He did not want protests from the Catholic priests. His own home adjoined a Roman Catholic mission station and he wanted to keep on friendly terms.

The pressure grew from many people of Gwassi. In desperation, the chief consulted the priest.

"They must stay out," the priest insisted. "The Elim people have already interfered with many of our churches and large numbers of our communicants have joined them!"

"As you say," the chief replied meekly and left.

The next day he reported to Henry. "Sorry, you are good people but you do not have permission."

Then an idea came to Henry. "I have one thing to ask," he said. "Since you won't allow us to start a church, give me permission for one meeting—only one. Then if you do not want me back, I will not trouble you again."

Obviously relieved to settle the tension, the chief agreed. The next day Henry and two evangelists traveled on foot across Gwassi Location, stopping at villages, informing the people of the coming meeting.

The appointed day arrived; more than two hundred people thronged to the open-air meeting place. Gwassi, one of the arid regions near Lake Victoria, has almost no trees large enough to provide shade. People sat in the hot sun at least two hours, listening to the preaching.

A week later the chief came to Henry. "All right, you have won. The people not only want to hear more of this Gospel you preach, but insist we give you a plot of ground for a church."

Then he stared at Henry several seconds and threw up his hands. "I submit!" But he grinned a bit when he said this.

Within weeks a preacher went to Gwassi, and a building had been started. The church flourished from the first week. In two months a second church opened, then a third. Before long, word spread back to the Catholic mission.

An irate priest drove up to the chief's house, honked loudly, then stomped out of the car, and knocked angrily on the door. "What have you done?" he demanded. "Why did you allow the Elim people to come into Gwassi? Did we not forbid you to give permission?"

"Yes, you did," the chief replied softly, "but you must also remember something. While I am a loyal Roman Catholic, I am also a servant of the people."

Surprised, the priest retorted, "This cannot be! We have already had too much interference from Elim! People flock to their churches!"

The chief answered (he reported to Henry later), "But can I do anything about it? They have given no cause for complaint. Men who used to be drunkards now work and even pay their poll tax. Two prostitutes have now returned to their husbands and worship in that church. Those who used to steal are now confessing, and we do not fear robbers coming to our homes at night anymore. Can I forbid missionaries to bring in their religion when it helps us become better people?"

The impatient, fair-skinned priest listened and shook his head. "No, no, of course not." He stalked out the door and drove away.

From that time on, we had no opposition in Gwassi, or any other location. The work flourished. Revival had come to Nyanza province and we were in the midst of it.

It always thrilled me to watch the Africans pray for healing. They expected results! Many times their faith far exceeded ours. The list of healings is almost endless; bodily ailments of every description and degree.

Deranged people often roamed aimlessly around the countryside naked. Most Africans fed them, offered them places to sleep, never molesting them in any way. I remember the first one who came to Suna. He ran across the mission station, wearing nothing but grass and leaves in his hair. He told me he was Jesus who had been crucified and was now risen from the dead.

I didn't know how to handle him. Seeing my predicament, Henry hurried over and led him away. Henry winked and said in English, "I want to feed him first, then we'll pray for him. God will deliver."

And He did! The man's mind returned to normal, and he left us the next day in borrowed clothes!

On one occasion, Shirley spoke at a women's meeting outside Migori. At the end of the service, the sick came forward for prayer. One woman, bulging from the waist was among them. She had been to the local medical center when she thought she was pregnant. They explained it was a tumor. She stood before Shirley and pleaded "Please!"

"I prayed for her and felt such compassion and such power," Shirley said to me that evening. "As I laid my hands on her I felt the Lord was already healing her."

But apparently the woman wasn't healed. For several days Shirley was disturbed. She realized God did not always heal, but in this instance she had had a strong faith that had given her the "assurance of things hoped for," as the Bible describes it.

Three days later, John Otieno, pastor of the Migori church came to see me. He spoke some English and often stopped in to borrow books. We had tea together, talked for awhile and then he got up to leave. "Oh, brother," he said, "I almost forgot to tell you. Three days ago your woman prayed for Druscila in our church who has a—a—(and he stumbled for the English word)—a—tumor . . . Yes, Druscila asked me to thank your woman for praying for her."

"John, Shirley was so sure the Lord was going to heal Druscila. She's been pretty discouraged over it."

John looked puzzled. "Oh, but yesterday the tumor passed through—through her body, if that is how you say it in English."

"That's good enough, John," I replied and then burst into praise.

"But why does your woman feel discouragement? Did she not tell Druscila she felt God was healing? And He did!" John shook my hand, hopped effortlessly onto his bicycle and whirred away.

Healing had its lighter moments, too. Sangra came to me one day at the mission when Shirley and Auntie Princic were at a convention. He showed me a large boil on the upper thigh. It had not come to a head but was inflamed.

"You must pray for me," he said. I prayed.

He waited silently after I finished.

"But—but where is the *sindano* (needle)?" (Meaning he wanted an injection.)

"Sangra, I have no *sindano*. Besides, I am not a doctor and couldn't give you an injection."

He thought about it momentarily. "Yes, I understand. Then give me other medicine."

I knew he would not leave without medication of some kind, but Auntie Princic had the key to our large four-by-three medicine chest. I didn't even have an aspirin. In our personal supplies I knew we had half a jar of Noxzema, some epsom salts and a small jar of Vicks Vapo-Rub.

"Okay, Sangra, sit down and I'll give you what I can."

I put some salts in water and had him drink that down. Then I gave him a half spoonful of Vicks (I had seen Auntie do that with dormitory girls for colds and they loved it). Then I got out the Noxzema, carefully pointing out that this *dawa* (medicine) had come all the way from America. The old man smiled approvingly. I carefully spread a thick layer of Noxzema over the infected area. He felt the burning on his skin and smiled again. "Ah, you are a good doctor, a very good doctor."

Three days later he sent his youngest wife (he had three!) with several eggs tied up in a scarf. She informed me that the boil had come to a head and been popped. But also, the old man had not had another moment's pain after I prayed for him and "treated" him.

When John Mark was three he came in from playing one afternoon. "I'm tired now," he said, throwing himself down. Minutes later, Shirley saw the flushed look on his sleeping face. His skin was hot. Quickly she took his temperature. 104°.

We both prayed, but his fever continued to climb. By nightfall it had reached nearly 106°. He began to go into convulsions. We emptied the ice cube trays and submerged him in cold water, then warm, then cold again. The convulsions stopped and the fever dropped slightly. We continued earnestly in prayer.

Then the fever broke quite suddenly. Within an hour his temperature had gone back almost to normal. Shirley spent the night on a cot next to his bed, checking him frequently.

In the morning he got up, ate breakfast and went out to play again, completely recovered!

Another time I became ill. I had been at Bukuria Mission planning a convention. About 2:30 I felt slightly nauseated and thought I would vomit. Soon the feeling passed and I felt fine again. My work was over and I jumped into the VW to head back to Suna.

I had barely gotten in the house when another wave of nausea hit me. I ran for the bathroom and reached the sink just in time! Then it was my bowels. Fortunately, it was the rainy season, the only time we had the use of our installed flush toilet and running water.

For most of the next four hours I alternated between attacks of diarrhea and a fresh attempt to vomit. Then I hit the dry-heave stage. Nothing stayed down. I became dehydrated. Shirley gave me ice chips to sip but as moisture accumulated, I started retching again.

We prayed but no relief came. I lay in bed, racked with miserable pain. Finally, near midnight, I put a blanket and pillow on the floor. I decided that my discomfort should not prevent Shirley from sleeping.

There seemed no relief from the constant barrage of pain. I could only toss and cry out for the Lord to heal my body. I recall glancing at my watch. With the flickering light in the hallway I could barely read the time: 2:35.

"Oh, Lord, please take away the pain!"

Suddenly a figure in white walked into the room. I could not see his features. I could not even tell if he was white or black. He came over and laid his hand flat on my stomach. The pain was so intense I was crying and rolling from side to side. But as that hand touched my stomach, instantly the pain let up. Within seconds it totally vanished.

I closed my eyes and prayed: "Oh, thank You, Lord, thank You!"

When I opened my eyes the figure had gone. The relief was so intense I could only lie there and continue to thank God. A few minutes later I crawled back into bed. I must have fallen asleep within seconds.

At six the next morning I awakened and realized I had been healed. "Thanks, Lord!" I was exuberant with praise.

But who was that man?

In my pain the previous night I had not even thought about him. How did he get in?

I jumped out of bed and ran to the doors. They were all locked from the inside, keys still in the locks.

Evangelists flooded us with reports of their ministries. Tobias Ouma wrote us:

> I prayed for a woman who had a disease in the back for two years. She was healed instantly. I also prayed for a person who had been troubled with pains in his stomach for six months and God healed him, also. Another person with back trouble was prayed for because he could not stand straight. When I prayed for these people, God healed them. They are all well and praising Jesus with all their hearts.

Wilson Amwago wrote a report which, after translation, reads:

> I went to a new place called Busanga to preach. Sixteen people found salvation and six were healed. We hope to start a new church there soon. One woman had suffered from stomach problems for four years. Then I prayed for her and through God's power she was healed. A man had a running sore on his leg but when I prayed for him, the sore dried up in two days . . .
>
> Another man had been ill for five years. He had much pain in his neck and had been taken to the

government hospital. He kept going back for three years, but nothing helped. When I prayed for him, the pain left and he is now well.

One man was saved in my church at Riagoro and it was so wonderful. He had lived in gross sin and everyone knew about him. He was also blind. Through prayer his eyes were opened and he now is really praising the Lord. All the people in his family have witnessed God's power and are now saved. There was a man whose left leg was broken but when he came to the church, I prayed for him and God healed him instantly.

One day I remarked to Wilson that I had seen many miracles in Africa—far more than I had ever seen in America. "Why is that, do you suppose?" I asked.

"Brother, I do not understand. I have little education. I cannot explain many things. I can only tell people, 'If you have needs, God will help you. If you want healing, God is the doctor.' I cannot explain, I only believe."

I drew my breath in sharply. "Wilson, on the contrary, I think you have explained."

God continued to work in East Africa. Numerically, Luo churches increased from forty-one in 1961 to well over three hundred fifty by 1964. All of Nyanza was affected, although we never saw any great outpouring in the Kuria area. From eight straggling churches in Tanganyika (later Tanzania), the number by 1965 had passed fifty.

But the work had its weaknesses, too. Essentially, our mission has been an evangelistic movement, putting emphasis upon conversion. It failed to give in-depth teaching. By 1965 the mission took steps to correct this deficiency.

Local training courses were held regularly in all provinces. The Bible school in north Nyanza trained more and more of our men. I organized and taught several short-term courses for leaders, and began work on a series of correspondence courses. Another missionary, an expatriate from Congo, then devoted full time to this phase.

Much of the initial work was financed by foreign funds. An African evangelist could start a church and continue as pastor for a period of two or three years, supported from abroad. But at the end of that time, the local congregation was expected to assume his total support.

It seldom worked that way. Africans are not used to supporting preachers. Furthermore, when a man went into an area he received twenty dollars or twenty-five dollars in American money. Monthly income of the people to whom he preached was less than four dollars a month! Local people depended upon their own land for food and needed little actual cash. Evangelists had to buy all their own food, except what their converts shared with them. Naturally, evangelists tried to keep opening up new churches in new areas, usually picking an elder or church member to keep the older work going.

Some men became evangelists for the money, and when funds were cut off, the preachers left the ministry. But some stayed—even when it meant great financial sacrifice.

Despite the failures and weaknesses, God worked! The revival fire was genuine!

15
Miracles

My mind boggled at what I had just heard. I stared at the woman in her ragged dress with faded patches. Her matted hair and dirt-covered legs told me she was probably either retarded or deranged.

"Go away! You are not welcome in my territory!"

She said the same thing again. *And in flawless English!*

We had come to Onyalo, a backward area near Lake Victoria, to help Otieno open a new church. Shirley played her accordion and Auntie Princic her guitar. Otieno had brought five Christians, all recent converts.

I walked over to the woman and looked into her eyes. Something indescribably sinister glared back. Instantly, I knew—she was demon-possessed. An eerie feeling swept me. My arms prickled; my heart beat faster. I wanted to back away. Except I recalled Jesus dealt with demons—even talked to them. I had seen Africans cast out evil spirits. I had had a few encounters myself.

"Satan, in the name of Jesus Christ, leave this woman!" I commanded in Luo.

"I cannot leave. I have been with her since she was a child!" the demon spoke.

"Let's pray," I told the crowd. The Christians bowed their heads, and I laid my hands on her head. Otieno also laid his hands on her.

We prayed for her deliverance from the power of the devil.

"Don't make me go. This is my home. I like it here." Each time she spoke in English.

We continued praying. She screamed and reeled backwards. Otieno caught her. She leaned against him, shaking and sobbing until she was able to control herself.

Then in Luo she said, "Thank you. For many years I have been troubled. Sometimes I would strike with my fists or curse people who came near me. I did not know what made me do these things. Now I know that I am free."

She later explained that she did not know English, and, in fact, could not read or write. *She did not understand any of the words the evil spirit spoke!* "I was standing there and the words came out of my mouth. I could not stop them!"

"Yes, but Jesus has stopped them!" shouted Otieno and he burst into a song, "Storm the Forts of Darkness. Bring them down!" And we joined him joyfully.

We were to witness other unusual happenings.

Shirley and several others attended a women's convention in a remote part of Karungu Location. An air of excitement permeated the convention.

"I'd never sensed such receptivity to the teaching classes before," Shirley told me later. "It was almost as though they had never heard about Jesus Christ. They hung onto every word."

Several women had never seen a white woman before. They came up, touched her red hair or stroked her pale skin. They laughed and teased about the softness of her skin and texture of her hair.

Between services Shirley chatted with three women who squatted, typical African-fashion, cooking over an open fire. Then she noticed a girl, perhaps twelve years old, who sat slightly behind the women, cross-legged on the ground. Extremely thin, almost emaciated, her face marred by terrible scars, the child stared vacantly into the fire.

"What's her name?"

The cook shrugged. "No name . . . we don't call her anything. She does not talk to us; we do not speak much to her. We tell her to eat, to gather wood, to bring the water, but that is all."

Compassion filled Shirley's heart. She looked at the pitifully deformed child, noticing scars not only on her face, but on her arms and legs as well. Shirley took the child's hand and lifted her to a standing position. There was no resistance and the limp body remained in that position as Shirley held her.

"I'm Shirley Murphey," my wife said, shaking the child's hand, smiling at her. "It is our custom to give our names and shake hands. I want to be your friend."

A slight glimmer of understanding penetrated the empty stare. The child nodded slightly.

"Come! We worship and then we eat!" called a woman from the church building. "By the time we have finished, the chicken will be nicely cooked."

Tugging at the child's hand, Shirley moved forward but the small form made no effort to follow. "Please . . . please come with us," Shirley pleaded softly, tugging again at the child.

Her head drooping, she allowed Shirley to pull her toward the church. They walked into the crudely constructed brush arbor, erected outside the church. The women, far too many for the small building, had brought small logs or carved stools to sit on. No walls, only grass and mats for a roof to ward off the glaring sun. None of the women seemed to notice. A cool breeze blew in from the lake.

Shirley sat down on a wooden folding chair provided for her. She lifted the nameless child onto her own lap, wrapping her arms around the child's dirty body and tattered dress. The girl seemed to be unaware of what was happening.

When Shirley stood up to speak, she carefully placed the girl on the chair, hugged her quickly and then walked toward the table which served as a pulpit. Twenty-five minutes later, Shirley returned to her place. The little girl sat stiffly in the chair, in the same position.

Later that day, one of the women told the nameless child's story. She had been born normal and healthy. When about two years old, she apparently suffered some kind of sickness. She had covered herself tightly with a blanket and sat in front of the open fire. No one paid much attention, assuming she had malaria.

The child pitched forward, possibly fainting, and landed in the fire. Her blanket caught fire, engulfing her in flames before anyone saw her. An older brother grabbed her limp body and managed to put the fire out by rolling her over and over on the ground.

She lived, although for days no one was sure if she would. ("Perhaps it would have been better had she died," the saddened mother mumbled.) Too far away from a medical center and with no money for treatment, the family had done its best for the child. Daily they rubbed her blistered body with oil and kept a net hanging over her for protection against flies and mosquitoes.

From that time on, the child never talked, moved listlessly if at all, and seemed totally unaware of anything around her.

During the three days of the convention, Shirley kept little "No Name" at her side. She held the girl, shared food with her and talked to her. The child showed no response. The first and second nights, the mother took the child away at bedtime, but both mornings she returned and sat by Shirley's cot before daybreak.

An hour before sunset on the third day of the convention, the final prayer had been given and everyone prepared to leave. The VW had been packed earlier and now only good-byes were left. Shirley hugged the little girl tightly and said in Luo, *"Aheri"* (I love you).

As Shirley opened the car door, several women came to her with gifts, following a custom which prescribes that no visitor should leave the village without taking something home. A few eggs, two dried fish, three fresh ones. Shirley thanked them for the kindness and got into the VW. The other women got in from the other side. As she started the car, Shirley saw No Name walk hesitantly toward them. She hopped onto the running board, reached up and hugged Shirley. In a forced, but soft voice, she said, *"A . . . her . . . i."*

Tears filled Shirley's eyes as she drove away. As she wound her way through dust-covered roads and grassy paths, she said aloud, "There is nothing the power of love can't conquer. That one word is the finest gift of all."

A remarkable women's convention occurred in Tanzania. Shirley went 150 miles into the interior with Wilfridah, an African women's leader.

At the end of the first meeting, Shirley started to leave the church. After a long, hot ride to the convention, followed by a two-hour service, she felt tired. She was hoping for a chance to rest before the evening meeting. She scarcely noticed the figure that came out of the shadows toward her. When he was five feet away, she glanced up.

"Efraim!" she gasped.

We had heard vague reports that our former headmaster had moved to Tanzania, but no one ever confirmed them. Shirley felt her hands tremble.

"Please . . . " she began. "Help . . . "

"Don't be afraid, Mrs. Murphey, I will do you no harm. I came to talk to you, please." His voice was calm and she relaxed.

"I did a wicked thing at Suna Mission and you were right to oppose me. I disregarded your rules every chance I could and even spoke against missionaries. We tried to get the girls to sneak out of the dormitory at night . . ."

Efraim's voice trailed off, and he stared silently at the red-haired white woman. "But now I have become a Christian. I am following Jesus Christ. About seven miles from here I teach a Sunday School class."

He paused again and looked intently at Shirley. "Can you . . . you and Mr. Murphey, forgive my sin? I have confessed to God many times. Now I wish to confess to you and to ask your forgiveness."

"Of course," Shirley smiled. "We've prayed so often for you. I'm glad you came today to tell me what happened. This is the best news of the entire convention!"

I rejoiced at the news. God had straightened out another sinful life.

I also felt a little smug. God had vindicated me at last.

I lost no time in spreading the word of what the Lord had done for Efraim. God had finally gotten to him and broken him down.

My turn was coming.

16
To the Masai

I consider myself a good judge of people, but I was wrong about Joram.

His father worked for Bukuria missionaries as a cook for many years. Joram followed his father and became a dependable and conscientious "kitchen captain."

Most missionaries hire an African to do housework, paying less than ten dollars a month. By having a cook, the wives spend the time in active ministry instead of in the kitchen.

Joram started drinking, however. He was fired after repeated drinking bouts, forgiven countless times and rehired, only to violate his promise to reform.

In 1959 Joram was fired again. "And this time it's final," the missionary said. Joram moved to north Nyanza. Four years later Christians from the Salvation Army met Joram and told him God would set him free from every evil. He had heard it all before—but this time he listened. One Christian in that group talked to Joram about his eternal destiny. The missionary became so burdened he spent the whole night praying for the drunkard and preaching to him the message of deliverance.

"I knew he cared about me. He refused to leave until I met Jesus Christ," Joram said.

The experience transformed Joram. He returned to the mission and asked for work again. "You don't have to worry about my drinking. Jesus has cured me. Now all I want is a chance to work." We hired him.

Joram began seriously studying the Bible. At church on Sundays, he would ask the preacher for a few minutes to exhort the people. In early 1964 we had a short-term training course for fifty of our pastors. Joram begged for permission to attend.

We granted his request. One morning during the training course he came to me and announced, "God has called me to preach to the Masai people. In a dream last night God called me by name and said I must preach to them."

Frankly, I didn't know how seriously to take Joram. I had no doubts of his commitment, but I did doubt his ability. He seemed too easy going, lacking initiative.

"Joram, keep praying for the Lord to guide," I said, hoping that would be the end of it. We needed a worker for Masai—but an experienced man. Joram had been a Christian such a short time, and I was certain his zeal had overcome his common sense.

He nodded and said no more about the Masai. For a whole week!

Then once more he told me, "Brother, I must go. God spoke to me again in a dream. I wish you to send me to the Masai. But even if you will not send me, I'll go by myself. *I must go.*"

I looked at Joram carefully. He was terribly serious. I still had some misgivings, but I did not want to miss God's will. I prayed momentarily. Joram bowed his head and prayed silently, too.

"Joram," I said, "why don't you keep your job here but preach to the Masai on Sundays? If, after a month or six weeks, you feel God is really calling you to preach, I'll do everything I can to get you financial support."

Joram grinned and then ran happily across the mission station. He started preaching the following Sunday! Every Saturday evening he left Bukuria (where we were living at the time), and returned early Monday morning. He walked from place to place telling the Masai about Jesus. Joyfully he reported the conversion of two Masai men.

"Keep it up, Joram" I urged, but said nothing about future ministry.

One Monday he said, "Brother Omore, I have now arranged a meeting for you to preach to the Masai yourself. On next Wednesday you will drive to the Masai in your car and take me. Elders will wait for us and you may preach to them."

I went. To my surprise, seventy-five older men waited for me. Most of them had large spears which they stuck into the ground behind them. Several sat listening as I spoke in Swahili. They stared blankly, their jaws moving perpetually as they chewed the native tobacco. The chewing paused only long enough for spitting on the ground.

After I concluded, Joram stood up and extended an invitation to accept Jesus Christ. Twelve men slowly rose to their feet and came forward. I was convinced; Joram had passed the test.

The elders gave their permission for Joram to work among them. He quit his job and a week later had moved among the Masai people. We also arranged for financial support for him.

Language presented a problem for Joram. Although he

spoke five African dialects, he did not know Masai. Few of the Masai knew Swahili well. That meant Joram needed an interpreter while learning the language. He found one—a Masai who had gone to school, but who was also drunk most of the time. The man agreed to interpret for Joram. At the fourth meeting, the interpreter was so drunk he leaned heavily against Joram all through the service.

Joram spoke slowly so that the interpreter's fuzzy brain could absorb what he said. When the message concluded—nearly an hour later—Joram extended an invitation.

The interpreter fell to his knees. "Pray for me. Pray for God to forgive me for my many sins!"

Within six weeks Joram had a small band of believers. On one particular day, Joram and a dozen people were going to a meeting. In order to reach their destination they had to climb a steep mountain pass. Just before they reached the plateau, they had to climb on their hands and knees. As they made the top, they could see rain clouds gathering.

We'll all be drenched, Joram thought. There was no shelter. Even by retreating, they would not be able to find protection before the rain fell.

"Wait!" Joram cried out, "we'll ask God to make the rain pass by and not fall on us!" Joram dropped to his knees and made his request. The Masai group gazed skyward as angry clouds approached on three sides. They could see the heavy downpour and lightning and hear the rumble of thunder. Joram kept praying.

"Look! Look!" a woman pointed. The rain was moving past them!

"Now I know you preach the true God," a man cried out. "Please pray that I'll never doubt Him again!"

By 1965 we realized the revival was in full swing upcountry and we joyously participated in it. Work among all the tribes except the Kuria was growing at fantastic speed. We had even seen a few sparks of life among the Kuria and continued praying for an awakening among them, too.

But we dared not rest. I was glad for Joram. There were other places waiting for the Gospel.

17
Broken

Evelyn sipped her coffee, leaning forward at our table. She, Shirley, and I watched the sun's slow descent toward the waiting mountains.

"That's one of the most gorgeous scenes in the world," I said.

"Yes, it is," Evelyn replied, raising the cup again.

After a few moments of silence she added, "I've seen a lot of those sunsets. Sometimes I hoped I'd never see another one—at least not in Africa."

Shirley looked at her quizzically, and I asked: "What do you mean?"

"I've had a lot of rough times in Kenya. Harder than you'll ever know," Evelyn said, so softly I had to strain to catch her words. She clutched her cup with both hands and gazed unseeing at the dregs. "A lot of hard times . . . "

We had known Evelyn since 1961, but we had never been close friends. A tiny woman, dark-haired and with large blue eyes, she had worked in Nyanza province. Her divorce put her at a disadvantage, however. Africans had little respect for unattached females. They accepted a single woman with only slight reservations; after all, they reasoned, she might get married some day. But a divorced woman was so uncommon they regarded her with suspicion. She keenly felt the slightest rejection.

In 1962 Evelyn visited our mission and stayed two days. The second evening, as we sat by kerosene light and talked of America, she poured out the story of her broken marriage. Both she and her former husband had served on the mission field in another section of Kenya. Her family included a now-grown son, who despised his mother because she had returned to Kenya when he felt he needed her at home, and a daughter, who married a non-Christian largely out of spite for Evelyn.

A few days later Oswego, one of the African pastors said, "I saw Sister Evelyn's car at your mission the other day when I passed. Is she all right?"

"Yes, she's fine."

"What about her husband? I heard that she had one. And does she not also have children?"

I answered Oswego's questions, saying Evelyn was divorced and the children were now in America. One was married and one was in college. I only answered his questions; I did not add the details she had confided.

A few weeks later Evelyn and her co-worker, Marilyn, came to Suna.

"Do you have to tell everything you know?" Evelyn demanded.

"What do you mean?"

"Did you tell Oswego about my divorce?"

"He asked about your husband. Should I have lied?" I

asked her. I was immediately on the defensive.

Tears filled Evelyn's eyes. "It was none of your business. You could have said that much, at least. Now everyone knows. This has badly affected my ministry here. You know a divorced woman doesn't have the respect other women receive and this will definitely hinder my progress with the pastors."

"I just never thought about it," I said, still on the defensive. "You never said it was confidential."

The two women looked at each other. Marilyn shook her head. "I suppose every conversation you hear must be stamped *confidential* or you pass it on to someone!"

"No . . . I never . . . just never . . ." I stammered weakly.

" 'Even my close friend, in whom I trusted . . . has lifted up his heel against me,' " quoted Evelyn.

The words stung in my ears.

"I'm sorry," I managed to mumble and walked into my bedroom.

Evelyn may have blown the incident out of proportion, but still I had wounded her and lowered the effectiveness of her ministry for Jesus Christ. That was hard to accept. My irresponsibility weighed on my conscience.

Other instances came to mind: reminders of careless conversations . . . snap judgments about others . . . caustic remarks . . . hot rejoinders. I confessed them to God and prayed for forgiveness, but the anguish didn't disappear. I had not intended to hurt Evelyn, I kept reminding myself. But that did not make a viable defense.

The next morning I apologized again, offering no excuse. Then I added, "I didn't sleep much last night. This incident has disturbed me more than I can tell you. I promise to watch my conversation from this point on."

That crisis passed but I felt troubled for a long time. It was not the last crisis either. I know now that God was determined to break me.

The work in the Suna area progressed well. Henry and other emerging leaders continually opened up new preaching points. Revival fires burned, but the fire in my own soul was dying down. That incident with Evelyn threw me into a state of depression and confusion. I still functioned and did all my normal tasks, but I could not seem to push this incident out of my thoughts. Daily other forgotten mistakes kept coming to my mind. Everywhere I turned I saw how my words had hurt someone . . . my quick temper had done great damage to God's work. The old will power and self-discipline seemed to crumble. Reading the Bible became a dreary practice, prayer a hollow experience. My preaching, while it brought results as before, sounded shallow to my ears.

So many times since coming to the mission field, I had felt like a martyr. I had traveled thousands of miles to proclaim the Gospel, but had met rejection, been opposed by other missionaries, and on two occasions had been threatened by death.

More than two years of missionary service had elapsed, and now I was seeing for the first time my own responsibility in many of these conflicts. Before, I had reasoned, after all, nobody's perfect. I had seen my trials as suffering for righteousness' sake.

That was true to some extent, of course. But I realized now that some of the situations could have been prevented. For example, the incident with Efraim turned out well—he did become a Christian—but only after both of us went through a great deal of anguish. Had my attitude been different, the whole thing might never have happened.

Fellow missionaries turned against me. I now saw many reasons why: my cocksureness, brashness, immaturity, my flagrant pushing ahead without concern for the feelings of others. For example, I learned Luo quickly and lost no opportunity to remind others of my fluency. And when I mastered Swahili, too—all in less than four years—people like Lee Nelson felt it keenly. I laughingly said on one occasion that I was challenging Lee to learn Swahili, but I suspect my underlying motive was to show off.

We had genuine revival in Nyanza province, and I sometimes (unconsciously I hope) flaunted that before other missionaries. I answered piously that since the Holy Spirit had worked in our area, surely He would do the same in theirs if they would give themselves to prayer.

These previous paragraphs have been difficult to write. My intentions, as best I knew them, were right. I worked with intense zeal. But lack of love and consideration hindered the usefulness of my work.

However, even in the failures, the Lord still worked with me. He used those experiences to teach me of His grace.

I have always had trouble forgiving weak and undisciplined people. Why couldn't Christians establish a daily, consistent prayer life? Why couldn't they get rid of bad habits? Instead of speaking up and hurting people, why couldn't they ask the Lord to help them keep their mouths shut? They had the Lord; that ought to be enough. Perhaps I needed my own devotional life to break down before I could understand the failures of other people.

"Lord," I pleaded finally in desperation, "I'm too tired to pray much or find help for myself. I need You to do something in my life. I can't do it myself any longer!"

About that time Shirley and I decided to attend the annual missionary conference for Nyanza province. The theme was Galatians 5:13, "Through love be servants of one another." *Maybe I need that,* I told myself. We asked God for a fresh touch.

At the conference, a newly arrived British missionary, Maurice Wheatley, spoke on love. I listened almost spellbound, as though the Lord were speaking directly to me. I became conscious of God's love in a way I had never known before.

God loved me . . . even knowing my sins . . . He loved me! I felt at peace at last. A new truth? Only an old truth impressed on me that day in a deep and new way.

Afterwards I introduced myself to Maurice and his wife, Joan. They responded warmly and a deep friendship began between us.

Some time later Maurice and Joan lent me a book by John C. Ryle, called *Holiness.* Little did I realize as I settled down to read it one day that this book was to change my life.

The introduction and first chapter deal with sin. Never had I been so confronted with the extent of *my* sin. The concept of "total depravity" (as the theologians call it), which means that the will of man by nature is only corrupt and his natural desire is for evil, became a reality. As I read *Holiness,* I could not get away from the sense of the corruption of my own soul.

I read and re-read Romans 7:14-25. Cec Murphey was pictured in those verses. He was the man who knew the right thing to do and ended up doing the wrong. Paul's expression, "Oh, wretched man that I am," fitted my condition perfectly. For weeks I lived in those verses, feeling God's hand heavy upon me and saying, "This is where you are now."

No relief came as I read other portions of the Bible or when I prayed. I was a sinner, unfit for God's kingdom, unworthy to proclaim His love to others. Constant scenes flashed to mind. Failures—in my interaction with Lee Nelson, Benjamin Maisori and hosts of others—haunted me.

I cried to God for forgiveness, yet felt I could not be forgiven. It seemed hopeless. I had known the right way, even known what God expected, and I had failed. I had failed the Lord . . . myself . . . the people I came to serve.

"Lord, send me back to America. I've ruined so much of Your work. Let me start over again," I cried over and over.

One morning in early March, I knelt by my bed. "Give me peace over this! Forgive me," I agonized again. Intellectually, I knew God always forgives a repentant person. But I had no sense of being forgiven.

"Lord, I can't even face myself anymore. I'm so weak . . . so helpless . . . help me . . . I can't help myself."

I struggled to my feet and then stretched out across the bed.

"This is the end, Lord. I can't take any more!"

I lay there a long time, my mind numbed and my body suddenly exhausted. Then I became conscious of a verse of Scripture ringing in my head. My body tensed and my mind, now instantly alert, responded as the verse came again, "How blessed is he whose transgression is forgiven, whose sin is covered."

Remembering that the thirty-second Psalm started that way, I reached out and grabbed my Bible. After fumbling for the right page, I read the chapter several times.

As I read, peace filled my heart. An assurance of pardon engulfed me. *Cec Murphey was forgiven and his sins covered by the love of Jesus Christ!*

Now I really grasped what God's grace meant!

I began to understand myself. I was a Christian, a child of God, but still a sinful creature. Without the help of Jesus Christ, the same wrong words would tumble out and the same wrong actions would result. But with His enabling, I could overcome and be useful in His service!

Does it always have to take this much pain and struggle to be broken, Lord?

18
Mending

"I'll never be the same again."

I really felt that way after God broke me. Life would be different because I was different.

I told the Lord, "You forgave me. I believe You've done something wonderful in my life. I don't expect to be a perfect human being, but I do expect victory. And it will only be mine if You make it happen."

During the next six weeks, three experiences occurred—three challenges to what God had done in the breaking of my stubborn will.

Each year Elim missionaries met outside Nairobi for a three-day retreat. Angry feelings had been building up among several of us. Grievances . . . unresolved conflicts . . . disagreement over strategy. This year was not unusual—but the feelings seemed more intense.

I understood our differences. After all, each missionary was a leader. That meant strong opinions—and often strong feelings expressed frankly. The mission allowed its workers wide latitude, and in each area the work had a different emphasis and direction. We grappled with our problems. Some we resolved beautifully. Some we handled expeditiously, but in the long run, unwisely.

For me, the tensions had built up mostly over minor things.

And most of the small things centered on Milton.

Milton had labored in East Africa fifteen years. He envisioned a nation of Christians worshiping Jesus Christ and reaching out to all lands. What a pioneer spirit! He challenged Africans to start new works, to trust God, and to forge ahead in the power of the Holy Spirit! He worked hard and got results.

But Milton also had a lot of rough edges that hurt people. I regarded him as a kind of spiritual bully. He tackled a problem, devised a solution, and doggedly pursued it—even when no one agreed with him. But he didn't stop there—he kept at the rest of us until we either agreed or just gave in.

Upcountry Africans began referring to him as "Ironheart" because of his strong will.

"When Ironheart makes up his mind, no one can argue with him," Henry said, shrugging.

My differences with Milton were of long standing. He had ridden roughshod over me, making decisions in his area that affected mine as well. Yet he had consulted neither Henry nor me. Several times he had made unkind remarks about me. When I had confronted him, he seemed vague about what he had really meant on those occasions.

During the early days of trouble between Maisori and me, Milton had not only supported Maisori, he had even said to me, "I don't think you'll ever make much of a missionary."

For the week preceding the conference, I prayed every day for myself, for Milton, and for a real harmony among all the missionaries.

"Lord, I'm primed. At the first opportunity I'll let Milton have it. I know the old Murphey too well. And, Lord, I actually look forward to telling Milton off. I need Your help, otherwise . . . "

We arrived at the conference late in the afternoon. Most of the earlier arrivals had gathered in the dining room.

"We can unload the car in a few minutes, Honey," I said. "Let's relax and have a cup of tea." Shirley agreed, for we had been driving most of the day.

"Hey, Cec!" boomed Arthur Dodzweit as he came toward us. He hugged me and then Shirley. May waved from the table where she sat pouring tea.

I greeted several of the other missionaries and headed for the serving table. Then I saw Milton. Our eyes met. I nodded and started to pass him.

"Hope you folks had a good trip," Milton said. The next moment he hugged me.

I couldn't respond to him. And I wouldn't pretend either. As he released me, I looked at his face.

Suddenly all the stored-up anger vanished. I must have stared at him several seconds. It was as though seeing Milton for the first time.

"Milt, I really *am* glad to see you." And then I hugged him.

An hour later, after chatting awhile and unloading our luggage, I lay on my bed. I silently thanked God for giving me a warm feeling for Milton. I had never felt that way about him before.

"Honey," I said as I propped myself up. "I had a strange experience in the dining room with Milton. I—I actually care about him. I mean, all the nasty things I wanted to say to him—they're—they're completely gone!"

"The Lord answers prayer, doesn't He?"

And I saw tears in Shirley's eyes.

"He surely does. And—and for the first time, I understand Milton."

I must have launched into a monolog then—about how Milton was a person who needed me to care for him. Beyond that aggressive facade lay a sense of inadequacy. He was a man who had set high ideals for himself but was never able to live up to them. That stirred him to even more frenzied activity.

I also realized that Jesus Christ had given me a love for Milton . . . a love that did not need to be returned. The Lord made me care—and it didn't matter a great deal how Milton responded. It was a step toward spiritual maturity.

During the rest of the conference, I felt a sense of unity with him. When we discussed strategy, twice I found myself agreeing where I had vociferously argued before. Once I challenged his judgment, but in a calm voice.

As I outlined a plan of strategy for work among the Masai tribe, his eyes narrowed—a sure sign that Milton was listening intently.

"Cec, I'll buy that. It wasn't what I had in mind, but I like your idea," he admitted.

Shirley, sitting next to me, squeezed my hand.

On our final evening we celebrated communion together. I discovered other missionaries had also cleared the air with each other. Another missionary and Milton knelt in a corner, and I overheard them praying for each other. A spirit of love I had never sensed before in our missionary gatherings now permeated the room.

I realized that Milton and I might have future conflicts. Both of us were headstrong and outspoken. Yes, it would probably happen. But I also knew that love would help me overcome our differences.

Two weeks later, the pastors and church leaders in the Bukuria area asked for a *baraza* (council meeting). The

Kuria people felt the Luo tribe had received preferential treatment—largely because I spoke Luo and the Luo churches had spread so far. Not as many schools had been started among the Kuria as in other areas. But the Kuria people overlooked the fact that the Luos vastly outnumbered them.

The grumbling had continued for months. The Kuria had rejected Lee's ministry. But they were not ready to accept mine either. Many regarded me with deep suspicion. It seemed now that the problems would be resolved only by meeting together.

Muhingira acted as chairman. Mwita, who had caused so much of the dissension, stood up. He listed their grievances—not once but several times. I bristled, awaiting my opportunity for rebuttal. As he droned on, I became acutely conscious of my anger.

"Lord, here I go again," I whispered. "That's my nature—to jump at the slightest provocation. Strike now and think later. And if You don't help me, I'll foul it all up again. I want peace and understanding with these brethren. You'll have to bring it about."

A soft answer turns away wrath. In my mind I heard it a second time: *A soft answer turns away wrath.*

That simple verse from Proverbs immediately calmed me. As I waited for Mwita to finish, I wrote the verse in a notebook in English, then in Swahili, and even in Luo. I filled a whole page with translations of that verse.

Mwita sat down. Everyone looked at me.

"Thanks, Mwita. You're probably saying what so many of the others feel, too. I *have* let you down. I have always tried to be fair, but apparently I've failed. Help me, brothers. Show me how I can change things so we can work together. We *can* have revival here!" I said earnestly.

Marwa stood up, repeated what Mwita had said. And I knew each pastor would, African-style, speak for himself even though the message was the same.

Marwa concluded, "Yes, Brother Murphey, now we can work together. We believe your words."

One by one the pastors spoke. And one by one they began making admissions, "We have not worked as hard as we should have."

"We were against you because you spoke Luo. We did not think you could speak their language and still care about us."

"We have failed to work for Jesus Christ as we promised."

That meeting pinpoints a change among the Kuria preachers. From then on I saw more cooperation. They began to fellowship with the Luo and Maragoli people. I saw no wide-spread revival among the Kuria people, but at least a definite forward movement began.

We closed the *baraza* by singing "Victory in Jesus" several times. And when we left the mud-and-thatch building, Mwita hugged me. "May God bless us both," he said.

Thanks, Lord, You're working. You're changing me!

Almost a month later, a third incident occurred. Lee Nelson came into my life again. Lee had been working in Jinja, Uganda, for several months. He and Helen had attended the Limuru retreat. So far as I knew, everything in the past had been straightened out between us.

Lee and I set up a joint African leaders' training course in Kisumu. He, Henry, and I shared the teaching with two leaders from Uganda.

During a session while Henry was teaching, Lee and I stepped into another room. We chatted easily about the course and the progress of the work in general. After a few more minutes I realized the conversation consisted of my talking and Lee's short responses.

"Lee, is there anything wrong?"

"Yeah."

"Something I've done?" I felt my heart sink.

"I'm failing in Jinja. What's wrong with me? Why can't I do anything but destroy?"

Lee talking that way? This was a side of him I had never seen before. He had always blamed the field secretary, his predecessor, poor African leadership, or lack of cooperation.

He talked on about the work. He lowered his head. At times I could scarcely hear his words. I sensed that God was breaking him as He had broken me only weeks before. I didn't try to share my experience—somehow I had not been able to talk about it to anyone but Shirley.

After he stopped talking, I took both his hands in mine. "Lee, I'd like to pray with you. You don't need my advice. I wouldn't know what to tell you anyway. I'd like to pray because *I care.*"

His head shot up. In silence his eyes questioned, "You really care?"

"Lee, I've been rotten to you. I'm pompous and always making a show of my linguistic ability. I've made it hard on you, but there's nothing I can do to change the past. I'm sorry about that," I confessed.

I prayed for Lee.

Then I said, "Lee, I want you to know that as the Lord helps me remain faithful, I'm going to pray every day for you—for as long as you're in Uganda. I want you to be the best missionary you possibly can be. And I'll do anything I can to help you!"

A few months later, Lee returned to Canada. He had not been able to adjust to working with either the Africans or the other missionaries.

I saw him at the airport and said good-bye. As he walked across the concourse, I waved several times, and I knew that I still cared about Lee Nelson.

"And, Lord, You made me care. Thanks for changing me. Thank you for giving me your love for Lee."

19
A Dream Fulfilled

On leaving Suna Mission, going away from Lake Victoria, one travels three miles to reach the crossroads. White markers point in various directions. Straight ahead leads to the Kuria people and beyond that to Masai country. The left fork goes to Migori, Kisumu, Nairobi and other large cities.

The right turn interested me that day. I followed the red, dusty-clay road for sixteen miles until I crossed into Tanzania. Only a small sign announces in both Swahili and English, "You are now leaving Kenya."

After crossing a brick-bottomed river bed, I reached the town of Tarime. One of the first things a visitor there notices is the houses—quite different from the roughly plastered mud walls of Kenya. Many houses have metal roofs, although more than half have begun to rust. Walls are made of dried mud bricks. A few were once plastered with cement but in time the intense rains have broken through the plaster.

One building especially, just as one enters the business section, demands attention. Solid concrete block, plastered and white-washed, it has a gleaming metal roof that reflects the sun's rays. The walls reach up only three feet and inside is a single room fifty feet by forty with a cement floor. The building has not been used for sometime.

On the trips I made through Tarime, I used to think, *Why shouldn't we start a church there?* For a long time I had prayed specifically for that area—and for that building. An opportunity had come earlier, but we could not raise funds for a preacher.

By the end of 1964, the door swung wide open again. Local Africans had visited our churches in other towns, been converted, and now pleaded for us to open a church within the city.

"This time . . . this time, it must work out," Henry said fervently.

"In the will of God, it will," I added with conviction.

After three weeks of protracted prayer, we found a source of support for an evangelist to work in Tarime! The Lord had really made the way this time. We began with open-air meetings in the public marketplace. Enclosed by buildings, it was the size of half a city block. Just as we started, we were informed that we needed a special permit to preach inside.

Undaunted, Henry asked, "But if we speak outside?"

The policeman shrugged his shoulders. "That is not my concern. I am told only that I cannot allow anyone inside to transact business unless he pays the fee for a license or shows me a special permit."

We walked to an open field across from the market; Wilson and Henry set up portable loud speakers and we began singing and preaching. Auntie Princic had her guitar ready, Shirley her accordion, and one African produced a tambourine. We were ready for action!

People listened. Young boys climbed eucalyptus trees. Others sat on the ground or milled around, looking into the amplifier. With accordion, guitar, and top-volume singing, we held open-air meetings every morning and afternoon for a full week. Each day we presented the Gospel and urged our listeners to turn from their sinful ways and follow Jesus Christ. Many responded at each service.

The official language of Tanzania is Swahili, although around the town of Tarime, the majority of the people speak Luo. We used both languages in all our meetings, not wanting to miss anybody.

At one meeting I preached a brief message in Luo which Henry interpreted into Swahili. This was an interesting exercise because I had been working hard on Swahili. Although I had carried on conversations, I had never preached in that language. I listened carefully to Henry's translation each time, wanting to learn as much as possible. One time I picked up the last phrase of his translation and inadvertently switched into Swahili without missing a word. Minutes later, I realized what had happened, stopped momentarily, and winked at Henry.

He grinned, slapped me on the back and said, "That's good, brother. Now you think in two of our languages."

That fired me up so much I preached another five minutes!

As Henry and I stepped back into the circle with the rest of the Christians, the accordion started a new song.

A man tapped Henry on the shoulder. "Who is that man?" he asked, pointing his chin toward me.

"He is our missionary—the white Luo. We call him Omore."

"Was he born here in Africa?"

I acted as though I had not heard.

Henry grinned. "Oh, no, he has been with us three years."

"Do not tease me like that! He speaks like one born to the language," the stranger said.

Henry laughed and whispered loudly, "It is because he loves us and has become one of us. Love teaches what schools cannot." He stretched out his arm and laid it on my shoulder. I must have flushed but it made me feel good. To be called one of them—that really got to me.

Yet in my heart I was not totally one of them—and never could be. The differences went beyond color. I could never shed my white culture and heritage; I had no right to expect them to become westernized.

When Henry and I worked together, we ate the same food and slept on the same beds. But when we returned to Suna Mission, I feasted on baked potatoes, roasted meat and salad. Henry went to his house where Margaret boiled everything African fashion.

Henry would have been as uncomfortable living in a totally westernized culture, with carpeted floors and air-conditioning, as I would have been living in a mud house with mud floors and grass roof.

But that did not prevent our working together. We were a team and there was mutual respect. By God's grace I had won the respect of the people. Perhaps they never forgot how I pulled up the flowers in the heat of anger—I'll never know, because no one ever mentioned it again. But they listened to me. I knew they accepted me now, not as master, but as a brother in Christ.

Few moments on the mission field held more significance than when I stood under that tall eucalyptus tree in Tarime. After the meeting I drew aside a little, looking around, thinking. A gentle wind teased the leaves. A few birds chirped and sang.

Tarime fulfilled a dream for me. I remembered that theater marquee in Chicago. The one I had seen years earlier with the blazing word: TANGANYIKA.

I had made it. I now walked on Tanganyika soil and spoke to people of that land. I knew their language, I understood many of their customs, and I loved them.

A sense of deep joy overwhelmed me and I wanted to laugh and weep at the same time. *It's great to be where the Lord wants me and to see a vision literally fulfilled. I'm in Tanganyika!*

No, God had not promised luxuries or good times; God had not promised that people would understand our actions or motives. But He *had* promised unfailing sympathy and undying love. I was deeply grateful.

Yes, grateful . . . to be a servant of the Lord . . . to be in Africa . . . to see the vision fulfilled . . .

I took out my handkerchief and wiped my eyes. The circle had re-formed; a new meeting was starting. Henry led the lusty singing. Auntie Princic strummed her guitar. A group of children sat in a row on the grass in front of us. I glanced up and saw that more children had scrambled into the eucalyptus boughs. Everyone seemed mesmerized by the singing, "Yes, God is good . . . Yes, God is good . . ."

Over and over they sang, from English to Swahili to Luo, to Kuria. The languages kept changing and the music rang on.

Yes, God *is* good!

> But God hath promised strength for the day,
> Rest for the labor, light for the way,
> Grace for the trials, help from above,
> Unfailing sympathy, undying love.